BUILDING
A
CHRISTIAN
HOME

BUILDING
A
CHRISTIAN
HOME

by HENRY R. BRANDT
and HOMER E. DOWDY

Published by SCRIPTURE PRESS PUBLICATIONS, INC.
WHEATON, ILLINOIS 60187

Building a Christian Home

by Henry R. Brandt
Homer E. Dowdy

The two authors of this book combine their experience in counseling and journalistic reporting to present this challenging study on the formulation of the Christian home.

The subject is organized into four separate and progressive steps — first, dealing with *you;* second, with the parents; then, with the whole family; and last, with the great task that yet has to be done.

A happy Christian home is not necessarily the product of two perfectly matched partners. The ingredient that so often is missing, or greatly deficient, is real Christian love. This can only be lasting within the framework of loving God and letting His love flow through the lives of both partners.

Eleventh Printing 1973

ISBN 0-88207-051-7
Library of Congress Catalog Card No. 60-53591

Contents

Preface

THE CHALLENGE of the Christian home is to formulate a philosophy to guide you in your judgments, help you in your day-by-day practice, give you reasonable understanding why your Christian home is unique. To this end has this book been written.

But with such philosophy as a start, you will have to be the one to study, to learn, to apply, to practice, to work at it if yours is to be a happy, well-ordered, successful Christian home.

We have organized the subject of the Christian home by considering first the individuals in that home. Each is a person who must answer to God and to himself for what he is. Then, we turn to the relationship between a husband and wife, discussing the mutually agreed on pathway they must travel if their marriage is to be a success. Finally, we emphasize the interaction between parents and their children. This pattern is basic throughout—the individual, the couple and then the family as a whole—whether the matter at hand is solving problems, meeting change or imparting sex education.

Vital to the understanding of the content of this book is that the reader know what we mean by "Christian." Basing our definition on the historic interpretation of the Bible, which we accept as the infallible Word of God, we believe a Christian to be one who finds joy and peace by submitting to the Spirit of God, who indwells him when he admits he is a sinner and receives by faith God's substitutionary sacrifice for his sin, even the Lord Jesus Christ.

Teaming of the authors has brought together the disciplines of psychology and journalism and the practices of counseling and verbal expression. Henry Brandt is the psychologist, hence responsible for the bent to probing the inner self. Most of the case histories, disguised enough to maintain confidences yet faithful to their actuality to be of practical help, are from his experiences. Homer Dowdy is the newspaper writer. He has had close association with the field of social adjustment through reporting assignments for a number of years. For the sake of unity and directness, the occasional use of the first-person singular refers to the psychologist half of the team.

This book has come about through long hours of discussion, pooling and filtering of ideas, and critical exchanges over each other's efforts at giving the ideas expression. We have a number of acknowledgments to make and we make them with heartfelt gratitude. First come our own families—Eva Brandt and the three teen-age children, Richard, Beth and Sue, and Nancy Dowdy and the five youngsters ranging from twelve to three years, Margaret, Becky, Barbara, David and Jenny.

Henry Brandt has been a pupil of Ethel B. Waring, whose ideas help form the foundation for the chapter on discipline. He has also sat under the teaching of Roy E. Dickerson, who was successful in instilling in his pupil his views on sex education and looking ahead to marriage, and whose philosophies are reflected in the chapters covering those subjects.

Both of us have known and appreciated David B. Treat for many years, Brandt as a former staff member of the Clara Elizabeth Fund for Maternal Health, which Mr. Treat heads, and Dowdy as a news reporter who has always found the Fund director a willing and helpful consultant in social-service reporting. His influence is ackowledged particularly in the chapters on sex education and growing with your children.

In an attempt to focus the most expert testimony in the field on the subject, we have dipped into the works of many persons, with footnotes to identify sources and to suggest further reading. We appreciate the kind permission of the publishers enabling us to do this. Of course, our prime source has been the Bible and we accredit to God himself any benefits that you may derive from this ministry.

Henry R. Brandt, Ph.D.
Homer E. Dowdy

Flint, Michigan

CHAPTER I

Laying a firm foundation

FROM THE ROMANTIC days of childhood we recall the story of the handsome prince who met the lovely princess quite by accident, won her heart and hand by the performance of a noble deed and, to supply a perfect ending, lived with her happily ever after.

The story is for innocent children, of course. But the thinking is often carried over into adult life that blissful marriage comes by some such fairy-tale formula. When fantasy gives way to reality, however, and we put away childish things, the magic of the royal castle vanishes.

Seldom, if ever, do the circumstances of living together transform the two people of a marriage into an ever-loving, ever agreeable, happy pair—fairy tales, popular love songs, and a gamble on fate notwithstanding.

A happy marriage involves a much greater challenge than simply finding a partner with whom you live happily ever after because of some strange chemistry that draws and

7

holds you together forever. Soon after the wedding day you realize that marriage is a test of your character.

Ken and Pat had a wonderfully happy courtship. They loved the Lord and wanted their marriage to honor Him. Ken enjoyed Pat's calm, easy approach to life. Pat appreciated Ken's decisiveness. "We balance each other," they said.

Very quickly after marriage they had some real facts to face. Pat snored and kept Ken awake. He was disappointed, never having realized that sometimes women snore. At times, he got downright disgusted.

Ken was the type who bounds out of bed every morning at the first ring of the alarm. Pat was a slow starter and had to be practically dragged from bed. Her calm, easy approach to life became annoying pokiness to Ken. He began to push and she bucked. They were consciously at odds over the tempo that their life should take. They were now "out of balance."

Ken and Pat knew that Christians ought not react this way to each other. They were willing to face the facts and the feelings, and prayerfully they worked out these early problems of their marriage. Ken sincerely prayed for grace to accept what he could not change (the snoring). They are working on the tempo problem. They realize that they do not automatically balance each other. It is taking continuous openness, effort, heart-searching, true repentance and self-sacrifice to keep their marriage in balance. They are seeking God's grace, patience and compassion for the task.

Happy marriage does not depend on one fortunate choice of perfectly matched partners. It is a lifetime process depending on many choices and many adjustments arrived at by two free individuals who deliberately choose the same harness and who continuously sacrifice personal freedom and self-interest for a mutually agreeable way of life.

The way you as a Christian respond to the challenge of marriage will depend on some unseen factors. These factors, taken together, make up the foundation on which your marriage rests. Time and again the shock waves of sharing life with another will reverberate to the very footings of the foundation, and whether your marriage stands or falls will depend on what the foundation is made of.

When discussing the Christian home and the marriage that gives it birth, what better time is there than at the beginning to look at the materials that make up the foundation? Simply, they can be grouped under two headings:

The declaration and demonstration of your love for God.

Acceptance of the Bible as the guidebook for your life.

If yours is to be a successful Christian marriage, it is imperative that the foundation of your marriage be composed of such materials.

THE DECLARATION AND DEMONSTRATION OF YOUR LOVE FOR GOD

What is it that binds two people together in marriage? You will say, "Love, of course." What you mean is a special kind of feeling, shared completely and exclusively by husband and wife and kept alive because of each other.

The Bible, too, says that husband and wife should love each other (Titus 2:4; Col. 3:19). But Jesus himself said:

Thou shalt love the Lord thy God with all thy heart, and with all thy soul, and with all thy mind. This is the first and great commandment (Matt. 22:37, 38).

If you give your undivided love to God, how can you give undivided love to your mate? It would appear at first glance that to love God in the way Scripture demands would be to relegate your mate to second place.

In writing to the Thessalonians, Paul makes a further demand on your love. He says:

The Lord make you to increase and abound in love one to another, and *toward all men*, even as we do toward you (I Thess. 3:12).

Does this not compound the quandary? How can you love God, your mate and all men and women? Or does the Bible catalog love as Brand A, Brand B and Brand C?

Something that Henry Drummond wrote in the last century may help us to see how we are to love. In a paper titled "The Greatest Thing in the World" he referred to love as described by Paul in I Corinthians 13 and likened it to light. If you pass light through a crystal prism, he pointed out, it emerges on the other side of the prism broken into its component parts—red, blue, yellow, violet, orange and all the colors of the rainbow. In just such a way Paul passes love through the magnificent prism of his inspired intellect and it comes out on the other side broken into its elements. Drummond calls this the "spectrum of love." It has nine components:

Patience _____Love suffereth long,
Kindness _____and is kind;
Generosity _____love envieth not;
Humility _____love vaunteth not itself,
is not puffed up,
Courtesy _____doth not behave itself unseemly,
Unselfishness _____seeketh not her own,
Good temper _____is not easily provoked,
Guilelessness _____thinketh no evil;
Sincerity _____rejoiceth not in iniquity,
but rejoiceth in the truth.

Study of the "spectrum of love" will lead you to understand that as you demonstrate your love for God you will be loving your marriage partner and your family—and, indeed, all men—in the very same love. You will not be loving God and your partner also, as if they were two separately directed loves, and others as if this were a third love, but you will love your partner and others all within the framework of loving God and letting His love flow through you.

Paul leaves no doubt about the source of such love. *"The Lord* make you to increase, and abound in love one toward another . . ." The Apostle John adds:

Beloved, let us love one another; for *love is of God;* and everyone that loveth is born of God, and knoweth God (I John 4:7).

Since God is the source, this love can be universally applied. It is spiritual fruit. It is to know no limits. It is broader than the union of two people in a marriage. Thus, it cannot be love that sets one man and woman apart as the twain that shall become one flesh.

If it is not love that produces the uniqueness of marriage, what is it? It is the relationship—the duties and details of marriage—that sets a man and a woman apart.

All of us are involved in a number of relationships. Some unite us with fellow workers in a job, with neighbors in a community undertaking, with other Christians in the conduct of a local church program. Each relationship has its own peculiarities, its own limits. Marriage is the most sacred and intimate of all relationships. But if love is a universal thing, marriage has no monopoly on it.

Does this mean that you are to love your neighbor's wife as you do your own wife? The "spectrum of love" says yes. Does this give thoughts of or lead to an illicit relationship? Of course not. You have the answer in the word "relationship." Love never got anyone into trouble. Relationships often do. You are to *love* all men. The *relationship* that binds you and your mate together is exclusively yours.

The relationship of marriage, however, is no guarantor of happiness. A husband and wife may live under the same roof, spend each other's money, sleep in the same room, eat together, give birth to children from a shared physical experience. But without the undergirding of the love of God, the intimacies of the marriage relationship can drive a couple apart.

To yield to the love of God is to produce a perfect love toward others, including the marriage partner. Conversely, faulty relationships are the result of a faulty relationship with God. A marriage based on sincere love for God can be disturbed only when something comes between one or the other of the individuals and God.

The trivialities of housekeeping nearly sent Peter and Sally into divorce court. She made the bed only when it was time to get into it again, seldom dusted, was a miserable housekeeper. He never was around when she needed help, let the car go to ruin for lack of care. Petty quarrels grew to bitterness. When seen against the "spectrum of love," their marriage surely did not measure up. Each came to realize, however, just where their smoldering resentments were leading and in repentance for their rebellion against God as much as against each other, both sought the love they lacked. Only then did they discover that prayerful, congenial discussion could lead to solutions of their problems.

Circumstances in a marriage change. Feelings do not remain the same. Physical responses vary from day to day. The thousandth kiss does not hold the thrill of the first kiss. Passion tapers off. If it did not, you could not stand the pace.

Because the old thrill is no longer there, a couple will sometimes ask, "Is our marriage doomed?" An individual will wonder, "Was I mistaken in my choice of a partner?"

You cannot expect today's reactions to be carbon copies of those you experienced when your marriage began ten or twenty years ago. You have changed. So has your mate. So have the conditions surrounding your marriage. But you learn to take these changes in stride because love provides the patience, the kindness, the unselfishness, the sincerity to cope with them.

"For better, for worse," the marriage vow reads. The relationship may lead toward either pole. The couple walking together in love will endure.

Our loving others, as we have said, springs from our loving God. You cannot love God without loving others.

If a man say, I love God, and hateth his brother, he is a liar: for he that loveth not his brother whom he hath seen, how can he love God whom he hath not seen? (I John 4:20).

And let us not forget that "We love him, because he first loved us" (I John 4:19). Such love should undergird all our relationships, whether with our marriage partner, our children, our brothers and sisters, our fellow employees or our brethren in Christ. It is this kind of love that is one of the foundation stones supporting a wholesome, happy Christian marriage and family.

Assuming you have declared your love for God, how do you demonstrate that love? By carrying out the "spectrum of love" in all your relationships, of course. But there is another important ingredient in your proof that you love God. The Apostle John tells about it:

He that hath my commandments, and *keepeth* them, he it is that loveth me . . . (John 14:21).

Your love for God will be demonstrated by the place that His commandments occupy in your life. You must study His Word to learn what His commandments are. This leads us to the other foundation stone of a successful Christian marriage.

ACCEPTANCE OF THE BIBLE AS THE GUIDEBOOK FOR YOUR LIFE

I have a friend who is an engineer. He has a thick book, *The Machinery Handbook,* on his desk. He refers to it constantly for facts and formulas that he needs to guide him in his work. Its pages are dog-eared from daily use.

Accepting the Word of God as your guidebook implies that you use it as the engineer does his handbook. If you do, the Bible will become dog-eared from constant use. In this case, you will be seeking the authoritative guidance needed to keep your marriage on an even keel.

Why do we begin this way on a seemingly elementary topic, that of the Bible as a guidebook? Simply because in years of counseling individuals and teaching Christian families I have found many, many of them to be seriously unfamiliar with the Bible.

To buy an expensive Bible, to carry it with you wherever you go, to speak of it reverently and to quickly read snatches of it in a form of daily devotions is not to make the Bible's contents a part of your life. Rather, to accept what Jesus Christ has said by making His words your own beliefs is to make the Bible your life's guide.

Jesus himself said, "If ye love me, keep my commandments" (John 14:15). Of His commands, Jesus said:

Whosoever therefore shall break one of these least commandments, and shall teach men so, he shall be called the least in the kingdom of heaven: but whosoever shall do and teach them, the same shall be called great in the kingdom of heaven (Matt. 5:19).

To follow the Bible as life's guidebook requires a familiarity with the commandments that Jesus gave and to keenly sense the place that they have in God's order. As an example, let us review what Jesus said about foundations:

Therefore whosoever heareth these sayings of mine, and doeth them, I will liken him unto a wise man, which built his house upon a rock: And the rain descended, and the floods came, and the winds blew, and beat upon that house; and it fell not: for it was founded upon a rock. And every one that heareth these sayings of mine, and doeth them not, shall be likened unto a foolish man, which built his house upon the sand: And the rain descended, and the floods came, and the winds blew, and beat upon that house; and it fell: and great was the fall of it (Matt. 7:24-27).

These totally different foundations call to mind two recent interviews that illustrate the importance of building marriage and the home on obedience to God's Word.

The first interview was with a retired missionary couple who had experienced much suffering during twenty-five years of working for God in China. In the midst of it, they had raised a family. Their home was a haven where serenity reigned. Husband and wife were considerate and kind and able to be reconciled when problems arose. They marched through life in the same harness. By teaching and example, they gave their children a happy home.

The children have now gone on to establish their own happy homes. After 50 years of marriage, much of it in circumstances of adversity, father and mother are closer to each other than ever. They can look back on a successful career, family life and partnership. They can because they listened to the commands of Jesus and did them.

You may say, "But these people are missionaries. It is their business to study the Bible. They have not had the economic, social and personal problems of the typical American family."

For rebuttal, sit in on this second interview.

The woman was a newlywed and already felt her husband did her injustices. She seethed over them, but kept her resentment as her own secret. Her marriage, she said, was starting out just like her folks' marriage had been.

Her father was a Bible school professor and was in demand as a conference speaker. He and his wife attended many social events, entertained a lot in their home. They were always thought of as a happy couple, so mindful of each other's needs.

But when they stepped out of the spotlight and closed the door of their home behind them, the picture changed. Nearly every evening ended in a fight.

"I often wondered how they could be such different people," the woman said. "They were the ideal couple when they were out and enemies at home."

He gradually drew into his shell and left the raising of the children to his wife. She would get angry at him for his easy ways. He would not argue. He just ignored her.

Finally, after the last child had left home, the breakup came. She had poured her life into the children. Now with them gone, there was nothing left. She could not stand him. She wondered how their marriage had endured for so long.

Those on the inside should not have been surprised. Here was a couple whose marriage had been based on pretense, conflict and bitterness. Does the fact of one's being a Christian worker ensure that when he marries one of like persuasion they will have a successful marriage?

The first couple was happy because they lived according to the way the Bible commanded them to live. Each was right in his relationship to God and therefore, as partner in a Christian union, was right in his relationship to the other. In the second instance, the husband followed the high calling of a Bible teacher. He taught the commands of Jesus to others expertly, *but he did not do them himself.*

The daughter realized it was too late to help her parents,

but she pleaded desperately, "What can I do to establish my marriage on a firm foundation?"

Jesus said that one house stood because it was founded on a rock—not only hearing His sayings, but doing them. The other house fell because it was built on sand—hearing His words, but not doing them.

To do as the Bible instructs you is to become a whole person. Each major life experience makes certain personality demands on you. Founding and building a Christian home requires you to possess certain traits and capacities in order to meet those demands. A serious study of the Bible will give you an understanding of what God requires of you for a Christian home and of the help He makes available.

CHAPTER 2

Establishing spiritual beliefs and behavior

THERE ARE REASONS why people behave as they do. These reasons are defined in as many different ways as there are people. If you would take any cross-section of Americans you would find people whose beliefs differ greatly, but their behavior is so similar that it is difficult to distinguish between Christian and non-Christian. If this be true, what necessity is there for Christian belief if an acceptable way of life can be achieved without it?

Mr. Lambert and Mr. Watkins are neighbors. Every Sunday morning Mr. Lambert takes his family to church. He believes that Jesus Christ is his Saviour and seeks to honor Him as Lord in all his ways.

Mr. Watkins also takes his family to church every Sunday. He believes that Jesus was a great teacher, the world's most

17

honest, good man. But he does not ascribe Him deity. For Mr. Watkins, Christianity consists of trying to imitate the life of Christ.

Mr. Lambert and Mr. Watkins work together, so they take turns driving. Neither of them would steal or cheat his neighbor. Both live clean lives. They would not intentionally harm their own bodies. They are careful of the example they set before others, are diligent in their work, handle their money wisely, give to charity, respond to human need, work for projects that contribute to the development of their fellowmen, would give their lives for the well-being of others.

In Flint, Michigan, where they live, a tragic tornado took scores of lives, caused much injury, and destroyed hundreds of homes. The call went out for help for the victims. Mr. Lambert and Mr. Watkins were among the thousands who dug down into their pockets for cash gifts. All told, nearly a million dollars was given against the financial loss. Then Mr. Lambert and Mr. Watkins gladly gave two days of their time, along with some 8,000 other citizens, to build 193 new homes for the victims. They worked alongside rich and poor, college graduates and the uneducated, Gospel ministers and unbelievers. All volunteered their help because the victims of the storm needed it.

Mr. Lambert, a devoted Christian, and Mr. Watkins, an equally devout religious man, have much in common. They work shoulder to shoulder, spend their money in the same stores, expect identical benefits from the schools, practice the same standards of conduct. Both have a strong sense of democracy and fervently uphold the laws of their government. Each is thrifty and tidy.

Commonly-held standards of conduct such as Lambert and Watkins share make little grist for quarreling or even for discussion. The "typical" American family, portrayed in literature and drama, is one permeated by common standards of conduct. So it is not strange that the Christian father and mother seem to be no different from the non-Christian in striving for such goals as establishing a home, providing family life, educating their children, providing recreation and social life and accepting responsibilities as parents, neighbors, citizens and churchmen.

They seem to be no different.

But are they different, the Christian and non-Christian? Are there differences between the Lambert and Watkins families?

The two families are different.

We are forced to conclude that it is not what they do that sets one apart from the other. Their activities are almost identical. Although their conduct is very much the same, there is an irreconcilable parting of the ways between these men when the beliefs behind their conduct are studied.

The distinguishing factor, the dynamic kernel for Mr. Lambert—and for all Christians—is, in short, his convictions regarding God, Christ, the Bible, man, the world, life, sin. These beliefs shape his outlook, his personality, his relationships with others. They underlie his values and the way he lets these values influence his life.

Teaching your spiritual convictions and their application to your children is the unique task of the Christian parent.

Years of counseling experience disclose that Christians who are wrestling for peace of mind are those who give lip service to their beliefs, but do not truly understand them or live by them. To live happily as a married couple and to master the task of parenthood, you must be clear about the makeup of man. For, time and again, a sharp focus on man's nature will be involved in your judgments about your family.

The Bible has much to say about man and sin. Two of many passages are quoted here:

As it is written, There is none righteous, no, not one: There is none that understandeth, there is none that seeketh after God. They are all gone out of the way, they are together become unprofitable; there is none that doeth good, no, not one Rom. 3:10-12).

For I know that in me (that is, in my flesh,) dwelleth no good thing; for to will is present with me; but how to perform

19

that which is good I find not. For the good that I would I do not: but the evil which I would not, that I do. Now if I do that I would not, it is no more I that do it, but sin that dwelleth in me (Rom. 7:18-20).

To summarize, these verses describe man (including you and your family) as having a knowledge of what is right and good, and the desire to do it, but there is within the tendency to fall short of doing it. Yet, you tend not to seek after God for help.

Mr. Lambert acknowledges this tendency, this failure to seek after God. Mr. Watkins gives no such assent, is inclined to deny it.

Is this Biblical view of man outmoded? It is no more old-fashioned than the views of some present-day psychiatrists. A comparison would seem to make the Biblical view up to date.

English and Pearson speak of men giving "lip service to Christian principles."[1] Man finds it difficult to achieve his ideals; "some force holds him back." He seems "unnecessarily thwarted"; he does not get "the right start toward a free exercising of his potentialities"; he becomes "fearful, doubtful, perplexed, in conflict, confused"; he has a "neurosis."

Dr. John A. Schindler speaks of the "sad reality in most people's lives." He explains it thus:

Behind the front they put on for the public, most people are disturbed; many are perturbed; others are worried to a point of confusion; some are frankly frustrated. Most of them do not feel up to par; they have a tiredness, a pain, a disagreeable feeling, a misery. They have a dozen matters they are worried about. They are brimming with apprehensions, fears, irritations. They have never quite connected with good living. They have muddled through their last 365 days, trying to avoid but always managing to stumble over new, nagging troubles, never reaching healthy enthusiasms, but going along nibbling on constant cares, irritated more often than pleased, timorous more often than courageous, apprehen-

[1]English and Pearson, *Emotional Problems of Living*, W. W. Norton & Co., New York, pp. 4–6.

sive more often than calm. That is the sad failure of billions and billions of people who have passed across the earth.[2]

These writers describe the effect of sin as they see it in psychiatric practice. They do not call it sin, but what they describe fits the Bible's description of sin.

The inner life of man does not present a pretty picture. In a recent issue, the editors of *Life* wrote of the "national restlessness," and expressed concern that even "decent, fed, adjusted, well intentioned" people will be in a poor state unless they "discover the internal quest for happiness."[3]

What others are vague about, or are groping to discover the answer for, the Bible clearly labels as sin, providing a not uncertain answer to what holds man back and causes a national restlessness.

Behind the glitter of our day, thinking men see a mass of people on the move seeking escape from a restlessness that becomes apparent as soon we slow down. It is important for us who are Christians to step off the mad merry-go-round long enough to ponder what man actually is and what he needs.

Mr. North was a beloved man. He had 85 people working for him and they always described him as the best boss they had ever known. At home, all was peaceful. He and his wife simply never had a harsh word for each other.

Suddenly, it seemed, Mr. North became very nervous and irritable. He developed a fear of his work, a fear of leaving the house. During the counseling process, we learned that for years he had been putting up a front. He had resented his superiors at the plant. Some of his employees had ways about them that irritated him. His wife had some habits that made him furious. But he had diligently kept up his front because he sincerely wanted to be the kindly man that everyone thought he was. But he could not keep it up any longer. He illustrates a man who tries to ignore his true nature.

[2]Schindler, John A., *How to Live 365 Days a Year*, Prentice Hall Co., Englewood Cliffs, N.J., 1954, pp. xiv, xv.
[3]*Life*, Vol. 47, No 26, Dec. 28, 1959, p. 69.

Paul recognized the wholesome desire of man when he spoke of "the good that I would." But he admitted, also, that man seems unable to achieve his desire. He laid it to "sin that dwelleth in me."

How do you go about overcoming that which holds man back? Schindler says that for the first time in history modern psychology and psychiatry have developed the "know-how for living." Maturity, he says, is the answer to the problem of only "fronting" joy and contentment. Maturity he describes as "a collection of attitudes" that work better than the attitudes a small child may have in the same situation. He defines an attitude as an established way of reacting to certain experiences. "The more mature a person is, the more complete is the stock of effective attitudes that he can bring to the great variety of experiences that arise in the course of living."[4]

English and Pearson observe for us that the frustration of pleasure needs early in life builds up a wall of hostility that later develops into pessimism, depression, indifference, lack of generosity, even active cruelty which "retard human progress and postpone the day of the better world."[5] How can you tear down that wall or prevent it from arising in the first place? They suggest that if the human being has a physically comfortable start in life, is made happy and has opportunity to express himself without too much unnecessary frustration, he is one who becomes optimistic, hopeful and can contribute something to the world.

These remedies run counter to the Christian's basic spiritual convictions. The solution to man's dilemma, the Bible teaches, is not in juggling the vagaries of environment. It is, rather, to turn sincerely to God and stretch out an empty hand and receive the inner strength to follow life in a wholesome way.

A doctrinal statement may read like this:

We believe that the Lord Jesus Christ died for our sins,

---

[4]Schindler, *op. cit.*, p. xxvi.
[5]English and Pearson, *op. cit.* pp. 5, 6.

according to the Scriptures, as a substitutionary sacrifice; and that all who believe in Him are justified on the ground of His shed blood.

We believe that all who receive by faith the Lord Jesus Christ are born again of the Holy Spirit, and thereby become children of God.

A study of the Bible tells us of the benefits that accrue to us through our relationship with Christ. He becomes our source of comfort and consolation (II Cor. 1:3-5), patience and joy (Col. 1:11), wisdom (James 1:5), righteousness (Phil. 3:9) and peace and hope (Rom. 15:13).

Mr. Lambert recognizes the spiritual poverty of man and says if he is to be helped, God must help him through the person of His Son, Jesus Christ. His neighbor limits Christ's help to the teachings that may be absorbed from Him rather than the benefits that may be implanted in the heart.

We have now, on the one hand, the Bible's explanation of sin as the cause of personal and family and even national distress, and of Christ's atoning death as the remedy for that sin and as the source of the inner strength to provide our families with the love they need. And on the other hand, we have those who place their hope in a good start in life, tearing down of frustrations and in effective attitudes, all apart from turning to Christ.

Which is right? Which works?

We know people who have lifted themselves by their own bootstraps. Watkins is such a fellow. We can also point to those who have been changed by the transforming power of God through the sacrifice of Christ. Lambert is such a one.

Can it be that they both work? Seemingly they do because both approaches are capable of controlling behavior. But behavior is an outward expression of a person. Outward behavior can be a direct reflection of what is in the heart or it can become an uncommon display of acting ability.

It is not a true indicator of whether there is joy and contentment in the inner life.

We all know people who are not Christians but who live in an exemplary way. And we have known people who claim to be Christians who are unhappy, unsuccessful, selfish and dishonest. The latter, if Christian at all, are not making full use of the benefits of Christ's atoning death. They could, but are not. They most likely are giving only lip service to their faith and in practice are looking for happy circumstances, good health, the favor of others, "the breaks of life."

Both can put on a front for a long time—perhaps even throughout life—but only through Christ, we believe, can one be enabled to conduct himself as he would from the heart. Paul learned this and in yielding to Christ found victory. Only by total surrender to Christ can personal frustrations be relieved and the national restlessness eliminated.

Whether one is depending on Christ to make him good (Lambert) or on his own best efforts (Watkins) is not observable. Since behavior may not be a true reflection of the heart, we cannot appraise a man by what he does. It is not our business to judge. We can judge only ourselves because we know in our own individual case if our conduct is a true representation of our inner self. One other thing is certain—God knows.

In choosing a man to rule over Israel, Samuel received these instructions from God:

> Look not on his countenance . . . for the Lord seeth not as man seeth; for man looketh on the outward appearance, but the Lord looketh on the heart (I Sam. 16:7).

Man can do a good job of acting, and the observable results may be no different from those of the person whose conduct truly reflects his inner makeup. But the heart of the actor condemns him. Only Christ can transform the heart.

Covering up your sin, instead of being freed from it, is a roadblock to making your behavior match your heart's desire. With sin forgiven and cleansed away by the atoning death of Christ, it is no longer necessary to put up a front, buoy up your spirits, do as people expect you to do, grin and bear it. No longer will you judge your life according to the behavior of others, nor set your values according to society's scale. As a Christian, you will order your life on the basis of your relationship to God. Not "what I want," but "what He wants." Not "my opinion," but "God's pronouncement." It will be "Christ living in me" as best as you can learn it from sincere study of His Word.

Rather than comparing people with people or being kept in perplexity by the philosophies of men, the Christian maintains his hope steadfastly toward God. As Paul put it:

> For it is written, As I live, saith the Lord, every knee shall bow to me, and every tongue shall confess to God. So then every one of us shall give account of himself to God. Let us not therefore judge one another any more: but judge this rather, that no man put a stumbling block or an occasion to fall in his brother's way (Rom. 14:11-13).

Is it not clear that an outlook based on the sinful condition of man and his need for redemption through the atoning death of Jesus Christ will give you a set of values that indeed are different from those of the non-Christian?

Here, in gist, is where Mr. Lambert differs from Mr. Watkins. If you accept this outlook, you cannot help but be different in your view of the issues of life.

Here we answer the question raised earlier, "What necessity is there for Christian belief if an acceptable way of life can be achieved without it?" Just remember, a life that is acceptable to others, to society, is one thing. A life that is acceptable to the one who lives it—totally and with complete satisfaction—is another. Simply, there is no acceptable way other than that based on the atoning work of Christ— none acceptable to God, according to His Word, nor one that answers that haunting quest in your heart.

One further consideration of the Christian's doctrinal

beliefs: It is his view of the future. One doctrinal statement puts it this way:

> We believe in "that blessed hope," the personal, premillennial and imminent return of our Lord and Saviour, Jesus Christ.
>
> We believe in the bodily resurrection of the just and the unjust, the everlasting blessedness of the saved, and the everlasting punishment of the lost.

Do you believe this? If you really do, such a belief will affect your views on the purpose and place of education, cultural activities, recreation, economic advancement and personal influence. It will have great bearing on what you value in these, on the use of your time and on your reaction to events in life.

Harold Johnson is a Christian who operates a prosperous manufacturing business. He says that all his business activities are identical to those of his competitors. He operates as efficiently as possible to make as good a profit as he can, has a good employee benefit program, studies the stock market and economic trends. He is interested in education, because his business requires engineers, accountants and other highly trained personnel. He puts a good part of his profits into a foundation, which is not unique, either.

But, he says, "my reasons for what I do are different from those of a non-Christian competitor. I do the same work. As a Christian, I do it in the name of the Lord Jesus Christ. I look for His return, when I will give account for what I have done with the talent He has given me. This world will pass away. For this reason, most of my money goes into a foundation to be used to tell men and women everywhere the Gospel. This is my major concern. I live for eternity, looking for another world."

II Peter 3:10-18 describes the coming judgment of God on the earth which, with its works, will be burned up. Peter then asks, seeing the temporary nature of this life, "what manner of persons ought ye to be in all holy conversation and godliness?" The Christian, he says, looks for a new order and because of this anticipation should be found "of him in peace, without spot, and blameless."

The Christian's values, then, are based on a knowledge of God's commands for the purpose of keeping them. The hidden things of the heart will one day be made known and all masks will be ripped away. The goals you have sought, the place you have given to things of earth and heaven, the way you have treated people, the motives that have guided you—in short, the beliefs and values by which you have lived, will be judged by God on the basis of your true nature, whether it is cursed by sin or redeemed by Christ.

CHAPTER 3

Focusing on adequate goals

THE CHRISTIAN's long-range goal, and one easy to lose sight of, is best described in Jesus' own words:

> I go to prepare a place for you . . . that where I am, there ye may be also (John 14:2b, 3b).

The ultimate objective for the Christian is not a good retirement plan to carry him comfortably through old age. The objective lies beyond old age and even beyond time itself. Old age is always followed by death and for the Christian death is the dawning of a new day. One unprecedented day we will see Jesus.

Our long-range goal, then, is to prepare for eternal life in God's presence, which will begin with that most eventful and heart-searching of all meetings, when we stand before Christ and "every man's work shall be made manifest" (I Cor. 3:13a).

Does this make us "other worldly"? Our citizenship is in

heaven. But we are to be in the world, although not of the world.

David and Janet decided there were more advantages for them to live in California than in the Michigan city that had been their lifelong home. A job was lined up, arrangements were made for a house. For several months before actually moving David continued to teach in the school where he had taught for some years. Janet continued her duties as a homemaker in the old house. But they often thought of life in California. They longed to be there, settled and in pursuit of a happy life in their new surroundings.

It could be said of them that they were in Michigan but of California. The Christian has his earthly obligations that require his honest effort. But they are to be performed in accordance with his goal, which is not of this life, but of eternity.

If eternity is in your thinking, it will direct your life and everything you do toward that destination. It will give focus to the training of your children. If an eternity with Christ is not central in your life, you will conduct your life quite differently. Peter, the apostle, said it very pointedly when he talked of creation being destroyed some day:

> Seeing then that all these things shall be dissolved, what manner of persons ought ye to be in all holy conversation [conduct] and godliness? (II Pet. 3:11).

Most people think about heaven now and then, but not everyone relates his daily life to eternity.

An intelligent chap with a good high school record came in for vocational guidance. He wanted to be sure his choice of engineering was a good one. All the evidence indicated he had made a good choice, and several courses of action were suggested.

A year later he was working in a factory, tied to car payments and going steady. A year after that he was on the job and married—and still talking about going into engineering. Four years from the first interview he still had done nothing about preparation, but still spoke of getting started some day. Here was a person who talked of a goal with his lips, but his heart led him along another path.

Likewise, the person who speaks of eternity with his lips but has his heart on other matters is deceiving himself.

Is preparation for eternity—involving not only escape from the consequences of sin but also a positive readiness to live with God—a conscious goal, something to deliberately pursue?

There are steps to be taken toward this long-range goal. Some of these steps involve:

Your own personal development.
Your relationships with other people.
Your attitude toward things.
Your attitude toward the church.

Let us look at them in more detail.

Your Own Personal Development

The Bible has a lot to say about the kind of person each of us ought to be. A careful study will point up the following benefits the Word of God holds:

It provides a clear understanding of yourself.
It is the guide to righteousness.
It is the guide to peace.
It is the guide to stability.
It provides substance for faith in the future.

A Clear Understanding of Yourself

You make daily use of a mirror because you want your personal appearance to be acceptable. A daily look into the Bible to see the reflection of your life is equally beneficial. The happy person is one whose outward appearance is acceptable to man and his inner life is acceptable to God.

In his epistle, James reassures us:

But whoso looketh into the perfect law of liberty, and continueth therein, he being not a forgetful hearer, but a doer of the work, this man shall be blessed in his deed (James 1:25).

30

A natural tendency is to skip the mirror of God's Word—at least the "continuing therein" part. It is easy to go your own way, following any line of logic that justifies a burning passion. You may use the Bible for any number of purposes, even as the source of a Sunday School lesson. But does the Word become a personal mirror as you look into it?

The writer to the Hebrews describes the Bible as a "discerner of the thoughts and intents of the heart" (Heb. 4:12). Approaching it with this attitude, you will be guided by the Bible into finding and maintaining a realistic understanding of yourself, your attitudes, thoughts, feelings and desires. The psalmist expresses the attitude that leads to understanding of self:

> Search me, O God, and know my heart: try me, and know my thoughts: and see if there be any wicked way in me, and lead me in the way everlasting (Ps. 139:23, 24).

Guide to Righteousness

A well-trained driver will almost automatically do the right thing at the right time in a car when under pressure. His "instinct" is a compound of knowledge and practice. In the Christian life, a knowledge of righteousness is basic to living righteously. Our source book is the Bible. As Paul puts it: Scripture is profitable for

Doctrine,
Reproof,
Correction,
Instruction in righteousness.

David said in the Psalms:

> Through thy precepts I get understanding: therefore I hate every false way. Thy Word is a lamp unto my feet, and a light unto my path (Ps. 119:104, 105).

If you are vague about the requirements for personal Christian living as stated in the Bible, you will do well to examine your goals. Do you want to live righteously? Do you want some day to feel at ease in God's presence? If you do, the Bible will tell you how.

Guide to Peace

A peaceful life is the evidence of a righteous life. A promise beautifully stated by the prophet Isaiah says:

> The work of righteousness shall be peace; and the effect of righteousness quietness and assurance forever (Isa. 32:17).

The psalmist said:

> Great peace have they which love thy law: and nothing shall offend them (Ps. 119:165).

Guide to Stability

Life is made up of varied experiences. There are times of favorable circumstances and times of trouble; stable and unstable times; surprises; varieties of decisions. The stable person meets life in a reasonably predictable, peaceful, and dependable way. In speaking of the righteous man, David describes him thus:

> The law of his God is in his heart; none of his steps shall slide (Ps. 37:31).

Did you ever hear of a man who had nothing behind his smile but his teeth? This describes the person who gives the appearance of happiness and a good adjustment to life, but whose outward manner belies his inner life. How can there be stability in one who thinks and feels evil but conceals his guilty conscience behind a pious look, who is filled with morbid misgivings rather than a real confidence in God? Of all people, he is most miserable. Such a clash between inner self and outward manner results in faulty judgments and unpredictable behavior. This person seeks to protect himself rather than to minister to others.

Instead of covering up sin—for this is what such behavior is—and pretending it does not exist, we ought to confess our sin and through the atoning work of Christ be rid of it, and thereby find courage and strength to face life. A peaceful walk is one that can be made only by faith in God's ability to provide for man's inability. When we walk by faith, Paul's testimony in his letter to the Philippians becomes our secret of stability:

> Not that I speak in respect of want: for I have learned, in whatsoever state I am, therewith to be content. I know both how to be abased, and how to abound: every where and in all things I am instructed both to be full and to be hungry, both to abound and to suffer need. I can do all things through Christ which strengtheneth me (Phil. 4:11-13).

Guide to the Future

The mature person keeps the things of this earth in proper perspective. Your view of life will determine many of your decisions and attitudes toward people, material things, future events. The mature Christian thinks in terms of eternity. Accordingly, his attitude toward this world is that all in it is temporary. He looks for Christ's return. His desire is to "be diligent that ye be found of him in peace, without spot, and blameless" (II Pet. 3-14b).

To achieve any goal, you must start with yourself. As a Christian you will strive to become the person that God wants you to be. What you are has real bearing on the other steps toward your chief goal—which you will recall is preparation for life in the presence of the eternal God, beginning with that day when you will give account of yourself before the judgment seat of Christ.

YOUR RELATIONSHIPS WITH OTHER PEOPLE

"Let your light so shine before men," Jesus said, "that they may see your good works, and glorify your Father which is in heaven" (Matt. 5:16).

You are confronted constantly by the decision to do good, or to cut corners, beat the law, cheat, steal, lie. With your goal firmly in mind, the decision will always be a simple one—good works. Others need the example of one whose immediate reaction to temptation is to do the right thing. As Paul said:

> Providing for honest things, not only in the sight of the Lord, but also in the sight of men (II Cor. 8:21).

33

A good rule of thumb in all human relations, even the home, is the principle inherent in Christ's words:

As ye would that men should do to you, do ye also to them likewise (Luke 6:31).

Here is a workable formula. And amazingly it is easier to carry out than to try to figure out the other fellow and treat him accordingly.

Lester Rhodes sought counsel because he was puzzled over his unhappy marriage. He and Vera, his wife, never exchanged harsh words. He kept his complaints against her to himself. He had looked at her personality, her idiosyncrasies from all angles and tried to do what would bring a balance between them. An interview with her revealed the same approach toward him. They never argued. But with all their efforts at adjustment, there was little happiness.

The principle of doing unto others as you would have them do to you was badly twisted by this couple. Their approach did not work because they simply could not figure each other out. Adjustments based on this faulty approach were bound to fail.

What is it that you would like men to do unto you?
Tell you the truth?
Ask you your opinion?
Help you in time of need?
Be natural around you?

Then do just that around others. When Lester and Vera proceeded on the basis of doing to the other what each wanted done to himself, their frustrations disappeared and they found a happy life together.

Jesus gave us another principle to follow in our relationships with others:

Love ye your enemies, and do good, and lend, hoping for nothing again; and your reward shall be great, and ye shall be the children of the Highest: for he is kind unto the unthankful and to the evil (Luke 6:35).

This principle involves the goal of seeking to please God.

34

Your treatment of others ought not to be in terms of their response, but according to your understanding of their need. It is God you serve. If this is true, their response is of little concern to you. You serve the unthankful and the evil as a service to God.

Matters between Mrs. Gregg and her daughter, Betty, were growing worse. Mrs. Gregg could not get the girl to study, do a chore right, play with her younger brother or even eat properly. Betty did all right when her father was around. It was a mother-daughter battle.

Did she not prove she loved Betty by self-control during their skirmishes? But almost without realizing it, she resented Betty in her heart. Indeed, she had made an enemy of her own daughter.

In a counseling interview, it was emphasized that she must love this little enemy when she was at her worst and the "hoping for nothing" part of the verse was emphasized. In time, she acknowledged her resentment was the problem and promised to give Luke 6:35 an honest trial.

"I'm sure your treatment was as shocking and painful as any surgeon's knife I've ever felt," she wrote some months later. "It has been less and less necessary to fall back on Luke 6:35. In fact, I am beginning to have a hard time remembering the mean, hard feeling I had toward Betty. Although I purposed to 'expect nothing' it has been impossible not to notice some changes that just could not be coincidence."

"Hoping for nothing" is a sound basis for your deeds. Then your happiness will not depend on what the other fellow does. Your reward will come from having obeyed God.

To seek favor through your deeds is to miss the mark. Jesus said:

> For if ye love them which love you, what reward have you? Do not even the publicans the same? (Matt. 5:46).

The initiative for kindly treatment of others rests with the Christian without thought of the response.

Peter spoke of the day when the earth and all in it will be burned up (II Pet. 3:10). In our day, with the emphasis on acquiring wealth, we ought to be reminded of this again and again. If the final goal is eternity in another world, then any accumulation of this world's goods for the sake of acquiring them has little ultimate value.

A man came to Jesus to ask what he had to do to gain eternal life. Jesus told him to keep the commandments. The man replied that he had done so from his youth up. Then Jesus advised him to sell his goods, give to the poor and follow Him. When the man heard this he went away sorrowfully, for he had many possessions. Jesus went on to say that it is easier for a camel to go through the eye of a needle than for a rich man to enter into the kingdom of God.

The rich young man loved his possessions more than he loved God. He had no desire to share them. Several men have come to me to discuss ways of acquiring wealth in order to use it to advance the Gospel of Christ. Two who outlined their plans have made good progress, but have become so absorbed in the task and so attached to their possessions that they have lost sight of their goal and become absorbed in using their wealth simply to acquire more wealth.

Some day, they say, their capital will not be tied up and there will be some available for Christian causes. Perhaps next year.

Jesus told of a man whose ground produced plenty. He planned a big expansion and eyed the day he could take it easy. Jesus called him a fool. He died that night. Jesus then taught this lesson:

So is he [a fool] that layeth up treasure for himself, and is not rich toward God (Luke 12:21).

The danger in setting riches as a goal is the risk of becoming selfish and losing sight of the fact that you look for another world.

The Bible tells us to lift up our eyes unto the harvest field, to pray that the Lord will send laborers unto the harvest and to go into all the world and preach the Gospel to every creature. Concern for the spiritual welfare of all men should permeate the Christian home. By your example, you can teach your children that the Christian is a servant and witness of Christ. If your world simply revolves around yourself, it should not seem strange that your children's world revolves around themselves.

It is important that children learn early in life the world-wide implication of the Gospel. Rightly practiced, the love in which Paul tells us to abound "one toward another, and toward all men" (I Thess. 3:12), will not be complete until it has moved progressively from our hearts and homes unto the most remote corner of the earth.

Where can the church go to recruit laborers? There is one place—the Christian home. And here is a goal for Christian families. You can do your best to make your children aware of the need in the harvest fields and encourage them to give themselves to the task.

The church in its broadest sense is the agency for preaching the Gospel, teaching the young convert, edifying the believer, recruiting and training workers. The church should be the major concern of every thinking Christian. Here is a goal worth while. Your wealth, your time, your children can be invested in this task, in preparation for the final goal.

By way of remembrance:

For we must all appear before the judgment seat of Christ; that every one may receive the things done in his body, according to that he hath done, whether it be good or bad (II Cor. 5:10).

Summary 1

The Christian home rests on an invisible foundation. It consists of love and adherence to the Word of God. Relationships are limited and unique, but love is universal. If you love God, you will love others. Without love, the intimacies of the marriage relationship can drive you and your marriage partner into separate paths. To demonstrate your love for God, you must obey His commands. This will lead you to a serious study of His Word. As you apply the precepts of His Word to your life, you will develop the characteristics required for good home life.

The essential qualities of a Christian home do not automatically come as a result of marriage. But the presence of these qualities in your family relationships helps make your home Christian.

We sometimes think of a Christian's values as spiritual, those of a non-Christian as something lower and lesser—probably materialistic and centered about self. Yet, those 8,000 volunteer house builders, while doing a very material thing, did it through a motivation that contained a quasi-spiritual element—a love for their neighbors and compassion for their needs.

Even among the worst criminals in our prisons are men who subject themselves to medical and bacteriological experimentation, with their own death a possible result, to make life a healthier and happier reality for mankind.

There are values that affect the way we make use of our time and money, how we educate our children, spend our leisure time and determine what cultural activities we will pursue. To approach these on a high-level, even moral (as against material) plane is not unique with Christians. Such an approach is shared by many regardless of their attitude toward God.

The difference that explains a Christian's values, and which he alone possesses, must lie elsewhere. It is not in the desire of a man's heart. Paul spoke a universal truth when he said, "for to will is present with me." Rather, it is in the acknowledgment of "sin that dwelleth in me" and acceptance of Christ's atoning death for that sin.

When faith is exercised in the efficacy of Christ's death, even the values commonly shared with non-Christians take on new meaning. Henceforth, they are viewed through the believer's relationship with his Lord. And where on the surface there was no difference in the outlook on education, family spending, leisure pastimes and the like, there is a difference after all, a difference that strikes at the very heart of the matter. It is a permeation of our values with the person and work of Jesus Christ.

Our Christian values and beliefs, undergirded by a demonstrable love for God and His Word, give us life direction and spiritual perspective.

As these values, beliefs, goals—this love of God and obedience to His Word—become a reality in your own life, you are then equipped to better your relationships with your marriage partner and others in your home.

CHAPTER 4

Understanding your roles

A PROMINENT BUSINESSMAN once came to my office to tell me that despite his phenomenal success in the business world he considered himself a failure at home.

"Why should I be?" he wanted to know.

"I have given my wife and only daughter everything they could desire—a beautiful home, each of them a car, an unlimited clothes budget. There is a trust fund to take care of our daughter's college education. I have never questioned my wife's spending for anything. Yet she is constantly complaining that I don't spend enough time with her."

He went on to explain that the three firms he headed depended on his personal attention to them. The standard of living he provided his family depended on the success of the businesses.

"What can I do when a customer comes from out of town? My wife knows that means entertaining. But I can't seem to get it through her head that the hours I spend on my business—and I admit I sometimes have a 15-hour day—are necessary or else she will have to give up what she has."

The time they do spend together, he said, usually ends in a fight or a deep freeze of silence.

"She's got my daughter against me, too," he said with one last sigh of resignation.

On the other side of the employer-employee fence is a factory worker whose job calls for steady overtime and whose spiritual convictions keep him busy in his church. He has been working nine and ten hours daily for years. He is a Sunday School teacher, deacon and personal worker. Few people will support the church's home visitation program so he gives himself to that, too.

His work is hard and his church activities take him out five nights a week.

"I come home bushed," he said during a counseling interview. "All I can do is melt into a chair. My wife won't co-operate by seeing the kids leave me alone for an hour. She is getting nervous and jumpy—complaining that she can't stand being both a mother and father to the children. When she gets upset, they do, too. Why can't she understand that I must work hard and long hours to support them? As for my church work, it is my one enjoyment and there are so few who are willing to do it. I feel it is the least I can do for my Lord."

Their stories remind us of a statement Socrates made about 450 B.C.:

> If I could get to the highest place in Athens I would lift up my voice and say "What mean ye, fellow citizens, that ye turn every stone to scrape wealth together, and take so little care of your children to whom ye must one day relinquish all?"

That ancient remark is strangely modern. It seems that down through the centuries man has been burdened to bring a healthy balance into his life.

The business executive and the factory worker were not faced with choosing between good and bad activities. At innumerable times they had to choose between two activities affecting their homes that in themselves were good. The more successful you become at anything, whether in finance or in teaching the Bible, the more demands there will be for your excellent services. Most people must come to choose not between the important and unimportant but among many good and highly important responsibilities and opportunities.

You should become aware of the roles that fall to you and study carefully how you carry them out in order to put your life into proper balance.

A good many people have achieved this balance. A young woman, mother of four children, says this of her busy husband:

"John is president of two companies. He is on the board of our church and also the board of two other Christian organizations. But when he comes home, he gives us his complete attention. He plays with the children, helps me when he can and wants to know all about what is going on in our lives. He expects me to keep up an active interest in what he does, too.

"At home, you would never guess that he has big business responsibilities and church and civic duties. He has to be away a lot, but no more than necessary. I am proud of what he does and do not feel neglected. Neither do the children."

ROLES OF THE MAN

Here are some of the roles that the typical American man must learn to keep in balance:

Husband	Neighbor
Father	Relative
Employer or Employee	Churchman
Son	Citizen
Son-in-law	Person

You may need to add some to describe you, or subtract a few. Which of these roles should gain priority? In what order would you arrange them?

Frequently the counselor is asked, "Which comes first,

my work or my family?" It is a sincere question and gen-
uinely puzzling to the one asking it, since he feels that his
family's welfare is at stake in either case.

It is our observation that the happy man is the one who
does not think of his roles in terms of priorities, with one
competing against another for a higher rung on the ladder.
Rather, he balances the roles, keeping them in proper perspective according to his set of values and the basic beliefs
that control his life.

Your life contains many roles. You may balance them,
overdo in one or more of them, neglect any number or
simply withdraw from those you do not choose to fill.

Which is more important to a factory executive, the
manufacturing of a product or the shipping of it? He balances them, of course, or soon he will have products piling
up or nothing to ship. If you think in terms of balance, like
the successful manufacturer does, then you must understand the function of each of your roles. Some overlap and
are not easily considered separately. However, for the purpose of study, we can look at these:

Husband

It ought not to be, but the role of the husband is a con-
troversial subject these days. Ephesians 5:22-24 says very
clearly:

> Wives, submit yourselves unto your own husbands, as unto
> the Lord. For the husband is the head of the wife, even as
> Christ is the head of the church: and he is the saviour of the
> body. Therefore as the church is subject unto Christ, so let
> the wives be to their own husbands in every thing.

A new day has dawned for women, a day of independence
and equality, applying even to marriage, some maintain.
On the other hand, many men give their own twist to
Scripture in claiming it gives them undisputed rule in the
home. Some husbands never get beyond the phrase, "Wives,
submit yourselves unto your own husbands." Others take
from the context, "For the husband is the head of the wife."

They overlook or reject the all-important phrase which follows, "even as Christ is the head of the church."

In the light of this tie-in with Christ's relationship to His church, what does this mean for the man in his role as husband?

He is to approach his role as Christ did His, "Take my yoke upon you, and learn of me; for I am meek and lowly in heart . . ." (Matt. 11:29).

Christ loved the church and gave Himself for it. A husband ought to give himself to his wife's well-being, dedicated to her even to his own death.

"For even the son of man came not to be ministered unto, but to minister . . ." (Mark 10:45). The husband has no cause to demand that he be served, but to ask himself, "What can I do to help my wife? How can I provide for her that will make her tasks easier?"

By no means is this an abdication of his role as head.

The role of the husband can be likened to the role of the president of a company. The executive must have the total picture in mind—financing, manufacturing, sales, employee relations. Of course, he depends on other people to keep him informed and to advise him. Co-operating with his people, it is his responsibility to help them work together smoothly, efficiently, happily, profitably. Perhaps he must delegate some of his responsibility for others to carry out. He must also have an eye to making preparation for the future. The company does not exist to serve his interests. Rather, he serves his interest best by serving the company.

At times, as president he must act decisively when a difficult decision is up to him alone.

In the home, the husband is responsible for the family. He should have the total picture in mind—financing, housing, training, planning for the future. He must depend heavily on his wife to carry out details. To do this, he may need to delegate much of his responsibility to her. At times, he must act decisively when a difficult decision is up to him alone.

44

The husband has the responsibility of setting godly standards for the home and leading the way by living up to them himself, just as Jesus set standards for His followers. "If ye love me, keep my commandments," He told His disciples (John 14:15). The commands of Jesus were not for His own gain, but for the good of His followers. A husband should rule his household according to the best interests of his wife and family.

Surely, this is possible when a man and a woman have been made "one flesh."

One more thought on the husband's being the head of his wife:

> If wives are to submit to the leadership of their husbands, every husband has the responsibility of being the kind of man that warrants submission. This is an appeal to your conscience. May you seek God's grace to meet His standard. Be done with mere lip service to the commands of the faith, and seek to experience the reality of what the Word of God teaches about your daily life together.[1]

Father

To father a child means more than being responsible for bringing a life into the world. To be a real father a man must do his part to train up his child in the way he should go (Prov. 22:6). Fathering requires of fathers their physical and mental presence, which produces direct contact with the children, and close collaboration with their wives. The head of the house surely ought to know, in a term today's youth uses, "what gives" with the children.

Leaders in the Big Brother movement know what it can do to a boy to be without the presence of his father. The boy may possess the love of his mother and even have a wide circle of friends. But with no father to take a big hand in his training, the boy experiences a serious problem. That so many boys with fathers are bewildered in growing up may be due in large measure to their fathers being present in body but not in spirit. When a father habitually carries

---

[1]Brandt, Henry R., *Keys to Better Living for Parents*, Moody Press, Chicago, 1958, p. 90.

his work home in his mind, whether or not he ever does in his briefcase, and is never able to shift from the role of a worker to that of a father, he separates himself from his family just as if he had absented himself bodily.

A father's relationship to his children is similar to that to his wife; that is, to be the head, but with his authority imbued with love. Paul presents a great challenge:

> Fathers, provoke not your children to wrath: but bring them up in the nurture and admonition of the Lord (Eph. 6:4).

Preston makes a lucid statement:

> Boys and girls acquire some of their attitude toward authority from their fathers. Both also acquire part of their attitude about the position a man should occupy in the family, about how a man should treat and be treated by his wife and other women, from the same source . . . If they have been fairly comfortable and nothing else has interfered, they use these same patterns in relation to their own wives and children.[2]

A father must never forget that how he performs his role may in a very real sense make or break not only his family but the future families of his children.

Employee or Employer

Men spend a considerable part of their lives working. Your attitude toward your work and to those who have supervision over you, or to those whom you supervise, is important. What a joy to be rightly related to your work and to those you work with. Paul says:

> Servants [employees], be obedient to them that are your masters according to the flesh, with fear and trembling, in singleness of your heart, as unto Christ; not with eye service, as men-pleasers; but as the servants of Christ, doing the will of God from the heart (Eph. 6:5, 6).

He has this to say to those on the other side of the table:

> And, ye masters [employers], do the same things unto them, forbearing threatening: knowing that your Master also is in

[2]Preston, George H., *Substance of Mental Health*, Rinehart & Co. Inc., New York, 1943, p. 76.

heaven; neither is there respect of persons with him (Eph. 6:9).

For those whose work is fascinating and a challenge to be met each day, their role of a worker can easily spring out of balance with their other roles. But there is no automatic release from this imbalance for those whose work is routine and whose conditions of employment are not inspiring. The boredom of a job or an attitude of griping can be brought home to interfere with family life just as much as a constant warning by Mother, "Shh—you mustn't disturb Daddy. He's doing his office work in the dining room."

And if for no other reason than that your work is your source of income, the hours spent working can vault out of proportion to the value that money should have in your family. The love of money and the notion that the things money buys are all important have meant shipwreck for many families.

The man who carries heavy responsibilities in his job may find it hardest to shift roles. The executive may call the signals all day at the plant or office and find on his arrival home that things are not going exactly the way he believes they ought. Perhaps there is little basic difference between the employer who forbears threatening and the husband who ministers to his wife, but the techniques to carry out each role may differ widely, and wise is the man who studies and then practices the methods that best help him fulfill his role of the hour. That such an effort is to be done in the strength of the Lord, rather than as an attempt to carry out one's best intentions, is, of course, a foundational premise.

To be successful husbands and fathers, men must shift gears when they get home. They must give their minds, attention and fellowship to wife and children as completely as they do to their work at their place of employment. A father to be really appreciated by his children should be just as quick to play with them or listen to their accounts of the day as he is to grapple with a problem at the shop.

Son or Son-in-law

Mother-in-law jokes are a part of the American tradition and usually are told by persons who are on good terms with their marriage partner's family. But any counselor knows that the pique of an in-law joke is not always in jest and that an amazing number of families are in distress because the wife or husband cannot come to terms about relationships with their own or their partner's parents.

Is it unreasonable to extend Paul's statement "he that loveth his wife loveth himself" to include also the persons his wife loves? And, as we said in the chapter on family foundations, to love God rightly is to love others, too, and that includes your own parents and your in-laws. Any couple, rightly related to God and each other, must come to mutual agreement in this matter. Relationships with your families will not be settled once and for all, but must be revised according to their changing needs and yours.

Neighbor and Relative

There are neighbors who borrow tools and there are neighbors who, when cornered in the garage, are willing to lend them. But to be a man who knows who his neighbor is, you must have the interests of others in your mind and heart. Philippians 2:4 tells us to "Look not every man on his own things, but every man also on the things of others." By this view of our fellowmen, we can anticipate and appreciate their needs and can fill the role of a true neighbor.

Your relatives can be considered in the same light for in this sense they, too, are your neighbors.

Churchman

Perhaps in no greater sphere can a man be an example to his children than in his role as a churchman. If you place high value on the church, your children will sense your deep love and devotion to it. You can demonstrate your dedication by faithful attendance, spending your money on it and associating with its people.

If you are a "church sleeper" or let work or golf or

"week-ending" come before the Lord's work, you can be sure that the value your son or daughter places on the church will be the same as they sense yours to be. This kind of behavior will almost certainly cancel out any high regard for the church you may have once planted in your children.

Citizen

Christians should be mindful of their role as citizens.

I exhort, therefore, that, first of all, supplications, prayers, intercessions, and giving of thanks, be made for all men; for kings, and for all that are in authority; that we may lead a quiet and peaceable life in all godliness and honesty (I Tim. 2:1, 2).

This implies an awareness and an active interest, with a high priority, in the affairs of government, the world and community organizations.

Person

As long as you draw breath, you will never cease to be a person. Children grow up and leave the home to establish homes of their own; tragedies can take loved ones out of your life in a flash; unexpected circumstances can change the course of your life forever. Come what may, *you* will remain to reshape your life.

A basic rule for everyone as a person could be:

Search me, O God, and know my heart: try me, and know my thoughts; and see if there be any wicked way in me: and lead me in the way everlasting (Ps. 139:23, 24).

Whether in a family of five, a factory of 5,000 or all alone, you must live with yourself. You should be the kind of person that you can like and enjoy being with.

Ted came from a Christian home and was raised in the church. War came along and before he knew it, Ted was overseas. There were no men of like mind in his outfit. Mail from home was scarce. Ted became lonely and began to sample the life that his buddies led. He started drinking and found some temporary relief for his loneliness.

One night he went to a bar with his buddies. The liquor flowed freely. It was a hilarious time. He became involved with a girl and later found that he had contracted syphilis. This was a great shock to him and caused him to ponder his ways. He was filled with guilt and shame and began to realize that even though an ocean separated him from his family and friends, he still had to face himself.

He recalled a passage in Philippians he had once memorized:

> Let your moderation be known unto all men. The Lord is at hand. Be careful for nothing; but in every thing by prayer and supplication with thanksgiving let your requests be made known unto God. And the peace of God, which passeth all understanding, shall keep your hearts and minds through Christ Jesus (Phil. 4:5-7).

Ted had forgotten what God would do for him. He had become absorbed in self-pity and as a result was powerless to withstand the temptations surrounding him. Repentance and a return to the Lord led him to a fountain of peace even in a faraway land, alone.

Then Ted found a friend who shared his standards. How he praised the Lord for His goodness. But one day his friend was killed and once again he had to choose to turn to God for comfort and peace, or turn back to the ways of the other men. He chose God, who filled the void and gave him strength.

Ted has since suffered other unexpected tribulation. But he has learned his lesson well. Whatever life holds for him, he knows he is still a person, one who must choose his ways whenever he comes to a crossroad and he will be personally responsible for his choice. It was Jesus who said:

> These things I have spoken unto you, that in me ye might have peace. In the world ye shall have tribulation: but be of good cheer; I have overcome the world (John 16:33).

What you are as a person will have great bearing on how you carry out your many roles in life. If you are a Christian, Christ is the one around whom your life revolves. His personality, therefore, should flow through your own personality into every role that is yours to fulfill.

ROLES OF THE WOMAN

Like her husband, a woman must keep her roles in balance if she is to lead a happy, wholesome life. Her roles include these:

Wife	Neighbor
Mother	Relative
Homemaker	Churchwoman
Daughter	Citizen
Daughter-in-law	Person

Some women will add to or substract from the roles in this list. We will consider only the roles of wife, mother and homemaker. Discussion of the other roles would be similar to the sections on corresponding roles for the man.

Wife

Sixty years ago, domestic life was virtually the only goal of a woman. Today, a woman can be as self-sufficient as any man. She has a wide variety of careers to choose from. Jobs are available for married as well as for single women. In addition, a vast world of clubs, social service and church work beckons.

The challenge of a varied life, continuous emphasis on the equality of the sexes, easy mobility and the telephone all contribute to making the role of a "wife" as difficult for the woman to keep in balance as the role of "husband" is for the man.

If Ephesians 5:22, 24 offers surprise to some men on the conduct of their role as husbands, the two verses in the passage applying to wives is something of a shocker to a good many women, Christians included:

Wives, submit yourselves unto your own husbands, as unto the Lord . . . as the church is subject unto Christ, so let the wives be to their own husbands in every thing.

These verses very clearly speak of the relationship between a man and his wife. She is to be *submissive* and in *subjection*. Somehow, many men and women in our day consider these words to mean disrespect, disregard for the interests and abilities of the woman. Thus, in deference to the democratic spirit, the word "obey" is eliminated from many marriage ceremonies with the magnanimous consent of the bridegroom, because to obey is an unreasonable expectation of a wife.

The terms *submission, subjection* and *obedience* take on a more positive meaning when applied to a business. Perhaps when regarded in this light, "obey" still belongs in the marriage vow and Paul's instruction is not out of date.

The relationship of husband to wife can be likened to the relationship between two banker friends. One is president of the bank, the other is first vice-president. They have worked together in this bank for 30 years. Only one of them can be president. Both, however, carry heavy responsibilities. The first vice-president knows the policies as well as the president. He helped make them, is in accord with them and is limited in his decisions by them. He can step in and take over at any time and the bank will go on as before.

The longer these men work together, the clearer and more firmly established become the policies. Freedom comes through *submission, subjection* and *obedience* to the policies. Because the policies are clear, there is never any doubt who is president, but the president depends heavily on the first vice-president to help carry them out. It is a friendly relationship.

Occasionally, circumstances arise that have never come up before. The president calls his first vice-president and other high officers together to ponder the question. It is a serious moment when a meeting of minds may be impossible. Such an occurrence is rare, but when it comes the president must make the decision, not according to a personal whim, but in the best interest of the bank. Once the decision is made, everyone, including the president, is bound by it. If, later, the decision proves not to be in the best interests of the bank, he will change it.

It would be foolish for these two friends to haggle over who makes the decision every time the occasion demands a decision. If there were feuds, arguments, pouting spells, double standards, we would call it a poorly run bank. Not so with these two men. There is loyalty, goodwill, confidence, deep understanding between them.

Neither of these men is limited to this one bank to exercise his professional skills. There are other jobs in other banks that are equally challenging. But they have chosen this bank. They concentrate on the job at hand. They are faithful. They willingly submit to the bank policies. Their decisions are in terms of the objectives and best interests of the bank, not their own interests.

Should not the role of wife be similar to that of the first vice-president? The husband is the head of the wife, but this should be on the basis of friendship, loyalty, goodwill. Family policies should be ones she has helped make, is in accord with, is limited by. We believe it to be a reasonable thing for the wife to be consulted and her opinions seriously considered when there is a decision to be made. Selfish interest has no place in a marriage. Both husband and wife must subject themselves to the best interest and objectives of the marriage.

Many women are brilliant, talented, able administrators blessed with good judgment. They should expect their talents to be used in the best interest of the marriage.

The husband as the head, with his wife equally dedicated to the marriage, should set policies and practices that bind them both. As the marriage goes on, duties and responsibilities of each should become increasingly clear and more firmly established.

Occasionally, circumstances will arise when a meeting of minds will not be possible. A couple walking along a mutually agreed-on pathway will come to a fork. The husband will want to go one way, his wife the other, each believing the goal lies at the end of the route he would choose. One must make the decision and the other yield, or the two will find themselves walking separate paths and the distance between those paths will widen as they continue on. Even compromise has its final point of concession. At such a time, the husband will carefully make the decision. We assume, of course, loyalty and respect and dedication between a couple.

When crises arise repeatedly that cause friction, we must consider that marriage sick and outside help would be indicated.

Freedom comes through *submission, subjection,* and *obedience* to a way of life that both helped to make.

Strangely, in our day a host of people think of freedom in marriage as complete individuality without leadership. All couples, soon after marriage, find that such a relationship is most difficult, if not impossible.

At her insistence, John and Agatha pledged mutual respect for each other's rights when they were married. In their early years, if he differed with her choice of friends, social life, style of clothing or religious life, she invoked the "freedom" amendment. "We must be broadminded, not imposing one's personal beliefs and standards on another," she would remind him.

Over the years John gradually conceded to her. Both became unbending, self-centered. She made her own life in parties, travel, fashions. He made his in business, civic endeavors, hobbies. They were clearly traveling separate paths.

But the novelty of new things wears off and Agatha began to feel the need for a companionship that neither money nor friends could give. She needed to "belong," to share. So she turned back to her husband, suggesting they do things together, asking his opinions about her decisions and plans.

Now John invoked the "freedom" amendment. He had set his course and did not care to change it. She is free to do what she wants. There is no praise, no blame from him. She has the absolute freedom of a lonely life. Now she does not want it. The foundation of this marriage is all wrong.

Husband or wife, when you come to a fork in the road,

whose path beyond the fork is to be followed? A verse reflects this question in a humorous way:

> A fellow and a girl who wed
> Begin to live as one, 'tis said;
> But many couples can't agree
> Which one of them they wish to be.

If you accept the Bible as your guidebook, then you as
the husband will take the lead and you as the wife will
give it to him.

Dozens of women have come to my consulting office because of a strained marriage. A chief reason for the strain
was that a difference of opinion arose in the marriage and
neither partner would concede. Case after case shows that
many women are not content even if their husbands give
up the direction of the home to them. Neither are they content to rebel. With such reaction becoming an established
pattern in wife-run homes, it appears that even with its
voice of divine authority laid aside for the moment, the
Bible has the common-sense slant on how a man and woman
can best live together.

Consider the beauty of Paul's challenge:

> Now I beseech you, brethren, by the name of our Lord Jesus
> Christ, that ye all speak the same thing, and that there be no
> divisions among you; but that ye be perfectly joined together
> in the same mind and in the same judgment (I Cor. 1:10).

In our day, the wife faces a major change as she begins
a marriage. She must often interrupt a career, a busy, fascinating, varied life involving contact with many interesting
people. She assumes the role of homemaker, which is a
startling change of pace.

Many wives indulge in self-pity, longing for their former
ways of life rather than proceeding to make the adjustments
that are necessary. But on the other hand, there are hundreds of thousands of happy wives. And not one of them
has a perfect husband! Experience shows that marriage is
a step up, not a step down, since the busy life of the single

woman can lose its fascination, although women not in this situation may find it hard to believe.

Submission to the task of being a wife is not the end of freedom, but the beginning of one of the highest and most challenging of professions. There is routine work in home-making, as in any profession. Think of the number of throats, ears and nostrils that a doctor looks into every day. Even the work of a newspaper man, which many look on as exciting, has its periods of quiet and its share of thank-less fittings of round pegs into round holes. We do not feel sorry for the doctor, because he does not feel sorry for himself. He is a member of perhaps the most respected of professions. Yet, he has endless routine work to do.

The wife, like the doctor, will become a contented person as she sees beyond the routine to the satisfaction gained from effective service to others, in her case, to husband and children. Self-interest is incompatible with effective service, marriage or parenthood.

One of the major tasks of a woman, then, is to study the role of a wife and keep it in balance amid many counter attractions.

Some wives will face the circumstance of unbelieving husbands or husbands who have stumbled in the faith. Among them are those men who are not only inconsiderate but act more like beasts than husbands. To these wives will come the need to ponder the words of I Peter 3:1-4:

> Likewise, ye wives, be in subjection to your own husbands; that, if any obey not the word, they also may without word be won by the conversation of the wives; while they behold your chaste conversation coupled with fear. Whose adorning let it not be that outward adorning of plaiting the hair, and of wearing of gold, or of putting on of apparel; but let it be the hidden man of the heart, in that which is not corruptible, even the ornament of a meek and quiet spirit, which is in the sight of God of great price.

If a wife cannot fully submit to her husband because of his unreasonable ways, she can submit for the sake of Christ, knowing that in His perfect love He will supply sufficient grace. The case is rare—and then usually one in which society must deal with a bestial husband—in which the wife cannot find happiness and success in her role as a wife if she is willing to work at it—or rather, to allow God to work through her surrendered life.

Mother

Is there a higher calling, a more challenging profession than being a mother? But for many women, the role of mothering can become all absorbing. In the opening chapter we mentioned a woman who became so absorbed in the task of mothering that she neglected to fulfill her role as a wife.

On the other hand, it is simple to neglect children, to make no effort to understand them, to be constantly fanning and keeping alive other desires that conflict or compete with mothering. This she can do with an over-emphasis on her role as a wife.

Preparation for a career begins in high school and continues into college for most women. This training must then be blended with the ways of her employer. Parenthood is like that. The woman brings her experience of family living to the marriage to be blended with the ways of her husband. When the first child comes, she is launched on a wonderful new career. Much is written about parenthood. Any number of older women have had a rich experience in mothering. The young mother (and older one, too, if she makes a serious try) has the choice of being well informed and expert in her field, or remaining a novice. Which is your choice?

Homemaker

To make a home is more than to keep house. The homemaker's program is to promote harmony and happy family relations and, in each member of her family, a sense of well-being. A homemaker's efficiency in doing housework is only a small part of her measurement as a wife and a mother.

57

Orderliness and organization are important, but Martha found out what Mary knew all along, that taking time to be a friend is important, too; in fact, that *being* is more important than *doing*.

COUPLE

There is a role which husband and wife share and which ought to endure long after the children have grown up and left to establish their own homes. It is the role of being a couple, the one which preceded parenthood and which they must maintain while rearing the children if they are going to possess it when the nest at last is empty again.

You will recall the case of the Bible teacher and his wife who separated after the last child was married (Chapter 1). This is no isolated instance. Why?

It was the children who kept them together. They had little else in common. With the last child gone, why stay together, why continue to put up a front? With Mother released from her mothering tasks, she faces the lure of charting her own life. Dad has worked to provide for the children. Now that world is gone for him, too. Although they may try, such couples cannot recapture the light-hearted day they knew before the children were born. In twenty years or more the tingle of just being together has given way to the numbness of the commonplace. Many play the role of parents so hard that they neglect their relationship as a couple. They allow themselves to become slaves to the children and strangers to each other.

A professor and his wife have made sure they will not look across the otherwise empty breakfast table some morning and ask, "What is there left now that the children are gone?" They make it a point once each month to get a sitter for the children and go off alone on an overnight trip, perhaps enjoying dinner in a romantic spot and staying at a hotel in a nearby city.

You may not be able to afford the luxury of a monthly honeymoon, but you can devise ways to keep your role as a couple intact and growing. Sunday School class parties for young adults and their children may be a fine family activity, but when they are on a "parents only" basis, they can be a part of the preparation for the day of the empty nest.

CHAPTER 5

Maintaining marital communications

THE SECRET OF good fellowship in marriage lies in two people applying the principle embodied in this verse:

> And as ye would that men should do to you, do ye also to them likewise (Luke 6:31).

Lester and Vera Rhodes (Chapter 3) found this out. Like practically everyone, each longed to be appreciated and have his viewpoint respected. They discovered that the rule Jesus gave is just as effective today as when He spoke it.

If you want appreciation and to have your feelings and desires count with your mate, then make a conscious, continuous effort to appreciate your mate and give due regard to his feelings and desires. When you and your partner approach each other with the desire to know, to listen, and to understand, you are ready to build a strong bridge across which two-way communication can flow.

The way to maintain mutual trust in a marriage is to be frank. Both the husband and the wife have the right to know each other's mind about each other, in fact about everything that concerns the relationship.

Such an attitude puts a high premium on communication. The term is used in preference to "talking," for people can do much talking and still live in a state of almost complete mental isolation. Communication means to overcome the desire to conceal feelings and thoughts and rise to the level of honesty about money, fears, wishes, motivations, sex feelings and responses, mistakes made, resentments and misunderstandings.

In seeking to build a wholesome marriage, there is a high premium on making a conscious effort to express your appreciation of each other—praise, if you will.

Jerry is a fellow who makes such an effort. He married Alice fifteen years ago. Just as in courtship days, he still expresses continuously his appreciation of her cooking, the way she dresses and combs her hair, her manner with the children, her spirit of sacrifice in her church work, her graciousness toward guests. She does not tire of hearing his praise. It is a pleasant part of life that contributes to maintaining good fellowship just as sleep, good air, meat and potatoes sustain a healthy body.

We do these things day in and day out, not as a distasteful, boring, dull, meaningless chore, but as a pleasant, helpful routine eagerly looked forward to because they are pleasantly beneficial.

It is important to know that Jerry is expressing genuine appreciation, that he is not just parroting empty, meaningless words his wife insists on hearing and he does not really mean.

On the other hand, Jerry also must continuously remind his wife that she tends to neglect housekeeping, spends too much time over coffee, which throws off the timing of meals, and leans toward extravagance. He does this most of the time in all patience and longsuffering. How much patience and longsuffering? Fifteen years of it, so far.

Jerry is a kindly man. He loves to be helpful to other people. Alice appreciates this about him and tells him so. She also keeps reminding him that she respects his faithfulness to his job and to his church, his thrift and his careful management of family finances.

On the other hand, she must keep after him because in his zeal to serve others he tends to neglect the children. He is careless, too, about shining his shoes and changing his shirt often enough. Alice does this most of the time in all patience and longsuffering. How much patience and longsuffering? Fifteen years of it, so far.

Why don't these people correct their ways permanently, you ask? It is a good question. We are not describing two angels, but a couple who have their strengths and weaknesses and who need each other. By keeping the channels of communication open between them, and with their relationship undergirded by deep love and a desire to please, each is a better person than he would be without the other. Yet, there is the tendency for each to drift back into old ways.

You do not get very far seeking to conceal your negative reactions, making excuses or seeking a scapegoat when differences arise. If the relationship is strained, you need to understand why and what can be done to improve it. When friction arises, it requires more than a description of the action that caused it. A careful sharing of how the act affected the quality of the relationship is necessary. The feelings, attitudes and thoughts that the act aroused must be mutually understood.

Keeping a marriage in tune brings to mind the story a father told about his two daughters. Both were given piano lessons and both were doing very well. Then the teacher assigned them a four-hand duet. Each child learned her own part flawlessly. It was in putting the two parts together that the trouble came, when it did come. Meanwhile the family endured the discords of their failure to achieve teamwork.

"Why not start over?" a harried parent would suggest. "If you both kept the same timing, your parts ought to harmonize."

And if a common feeling for the rhythm flowed between the girls, the tones they produced were a joy to hear.

A sense of unity between two or more people who function together is priceless, whether it produces the music of a stirring symphony or the steam-rolling tactics of a seasoned football squad.

We speak of teamwork, united action, agreement, intimacy. The essence of democracy is the voluntary commitment of free peoples to a way of life arrived at by mutual consent. One writer describes freedom as the length of the leash from a chosen stake.

The Apostle Paul offered a beautiful definition of teamwork in writing to the Corinthians:

> Now I beseech you, brethren, by the name of our Lord Jesus Christ, that ye all speak the same thing, and that there be no divisions among you; but that ye be perfectly joined together in the same mind and in the same judgment (I Cor. 1:10).

Fellowship, which amounts to comfortable relationships, springs from mutual faith, viewpoints agreed on, activities approved of and that overworked but nonetheless descriptive word, togetherness.

Opposite these terms are such words as division, contention, strife, disagreement, selfishness. Governments, churches and families seek to eliminate such conditions from their midst. The late John Foster Dulles was dedicated to seeking out "areas of agreement" among nations.

To be "perfectly joined together in the same mind and in the same judgment"—is there a more wholesome endeavor to give yourself to? This is the objective, the challenge, for the Christian family.

But in your effort to maintain congeniality in your family, one factor in human relations must be consciously and deliberately guarded against: *We tend to grow apart.*

Isaiah describes man in this way:

All we like sheep have gone astray; we have turned every one *to his own way;* and the Lord hath laid on him the iniquity of us all (Isa. 53:6).

We have turned every one to his own way—this is the story of two or more people living together. Jerry and Alice illustrate this. In the preceding chapter we spoke of an inevitable fork in the road and how easy it is for husband and wife to take up divergent paths. Nations make treaties, governments pass laws, young lovers pledge agreements, families set rules. In all these efforts we see attempts to correct the tendency to wander from a standard, to go our separate ways.

The Prophet Amos asks the question, "Can two walk together, except they be agreed?" (Amos 3:3). The psalmist reflects, "Behold, how good and how pleasant it is for brethren to dwell together in unity!" (Ps. 133:1).

Probably no one in the field of human relations would dispute the prophet and the psalmist. The battleground comes in the process of arriving at this unity and in adhering to the standard that maintains it. There are many shades of opinion on the standards, the values and the goals by which we should steer our lives.

Whenever two or more persons living side by side differ over a point, some kind of agreement must be reached, or there is a parting of the ways and each is the loser for it.

Carl walked into my office and slumped into a chair, a dejected soul. He was a success financially. But after 22 years of marriage, he was ready to quit, thoroughly disgusted with his wife. He had given up hunting and fishing because she did not like him doing them. They had no social life because she did not like to go out. They never fought. They just did not talk, but the silence was driving him mad. He wanted to go out, but felt guilty if he did.

Rhea, his wife, shared his attitude. She was a very bitter woman and looked it.

"I can hardly stand the sight of him," she said. "We have nothing to talk about. We used to visit his friends, but he didn't like the way I talked to them. He didn't say much, just gave me that withering look. So I quit talking. What's the use of just sitting? I quit going out. I don't like fishing and hunting. I don't care if he goes, but he thinks I don't want him to go, I guess. He's never asked me how I feel."

These two people, intelligent, polished and successful separately, are like the two girls playing a duet. When they sensed discord, each quit rather than work it out. Their marriage slowly ground to a halt. They were strangers to each other, isolated mentally and separated by an invisible but real barrier of resentment.

Now, however, they are on a friendly basis after having started to build a bridge of communication between them. It has enabled them to define their differences and work out mutually agreeable solutions rather than turning away from each other when signs of discord appear.

Each had been sure that to be honest with the other about feelings and opinions would blow the marriage sky-high. Instead, each found that repentance before God and drawing on His love gave them the grace necessary to begin building a mutual life.

This couple, too, illustrates the tendency to turn "every one to his own way." We tend to grow apart more naturally than toward an open, honest sharing of viewpoints, attitudes and feelings.

Judge John Warren Hill of New York Domestic Relations Court recently reported on 250,000 cases of marital failure that have come before the court. His experience leads him to the conclusion that "bottled up resentments constitute one of the greatest dangers to marriage."[1] His formula? *Talk it out.* He says that frank talk will do nothing but good, even though your initial response may be shock and wounded pride. He does make an important qualification—the marriage must be based on a firm foundation of love and unselfishness.

Hugo A. Bourdeau, a Baltimore marriage counselor, is convinced that the inability of husbands and wives to talk

---

[1]Hill, John Warren, "Talk It Out," *This Week,* March 9, 1958.

to each other is our "No. 1" marriage problem. He says the inability to converse shows up in 85 of every 100 couples visiting marriage counselors. Bourdeau points out that, during courtship, couples spend hours together sharing attitudes and planning for the future. But he would agree that in some of the homes they set up, the wife's easy conversation freezes into a mystifying silence and the husband's tender murmurings of courtship days develop the full lung-power of near raving.

A happy marriage is not possible without communication which reveals, with reasonable certainty, how the other feels about a given action or situation.

Bourdeau says:

> Without communication, there can be no adjustment at all. Ability to converse on any subject, to air any problem which might arise, to share with the other the private fears and worries and desires is the bedrock of marriage. And it isn't always verbal. Attitudes are expressed by a smile, a frown, a shrug of the shoulders. These are powerful. We *sense* disapproval even though the spoken words are reassuring.[2]

He goes on to point out that communication ceases when the need to conceal becomes stronger than the desire for unity. There is the husband who cannot speak of his financial worries, so he hides his insecurity behind what he calls a "manly" silence. The wife conceals her spur-of-the-moment purchase or keeps to herself the concern that her husband no longer finds her to be attractive. Slowly, couples who once were excellent companions learn to rope off areas of their lives and live in a kind of marital no man's land. Conversation declines to "truce" subjects.

But Dr. James H. S. Bossard, a noted sociologist, discovered that talking, alone, may get nowhere. By using tape recorders, he obtained samples of dinner conversations of Philadelphia families.[3] His conclusion? The way parents talk to their children and to each other in front of their children is a problem of great seriousness in family life.

[2]Bourdeau, Hugo A., "We Can't Talk to Each Other," *Coronet*, July, 1959, pp. 114-118.
[3]Bossard, James, "Danger on Your Lips," *American Weekly*, June 7, 1959, p. 2.

He discovered that family conversations follow certain patterns. The pattern of criticism was one of the most prevalent of those recorded. The negative atmosphere it created made the children anti-social and unpopular. In another, hostilities were turned inward, with quarreling the result. More subtly harmful were the exhibitionists, with each member of the family forever battling for the limelight.

Does anyone have good conversational habits? Yes, reported Bossard. He calls the right way the interpretive pattern. Here, persons and events are discussed calmly, with perspective and dignity, and when appropriate, with humor. Children are encouraged to take part and are treated with respect. Understanding and a wide range of interests are the characteristics of such a family.

The judge speaks of bottled-up resentments, a refusal to communicate. Bourdeau warns of the natural tendency for communication to break down as a married couple evolves slowly into self-protection rather than mutual helpfulness. Bossard points out that family conversation tends to drift in critical, self-seeking directions.

What are the solutions these men propose to mend the broken lines of communication between husbands and among members of a family?

Reveal yourself, they say; know, don't guess at what the other fellow is trying to say. Become aware of what you are doing, consciously take steps to correct any faults. Fall back on "safe" topics as a retreat.

Is there a Biblical viewpoint on the dangers these men have pointed out?

It is our observation that the Christian who brings his marriage problems to a counselor presents exactly the same kind of problems as these men describe. This again points to the conclusion that all men are grappling with the same problems and describe them essentially the same way. The Christian answer, however, plumbs far deeper than conduct and a concerted effort to get along. It goes to the very nature of man.

Let us look just a little further at the elements that cause our communication to break down. There is the tendency to hide. Jesus said:

> This is the condemnation, that light is come into the world, and men loved darkness rather than light, because their deeds were evil. For every one that doeth evil hateth the light, neither cometh to the light, lest his deeds should be reproved (John 3:19, 20).

Is it not true that we seek to protect ourselves from disapproval, that we hesitate to reveal our own selfish desires and tend to conceal our negative feelings? Yes, the tendency to conceal that is so aptly described by Bourdeau, is summed up in two sentences by the Lord Jesus Christ. Bourdeau presents nothing new—simply restates the pronouncement Jesus made to Nicodemus many years ago.

Again, the tendency for human relations to break down is described by Isaiah when he says, "we have turned every one to his own way." True, we have a strong desire for fellowship, but the human heart with its deceitfulness drives us apart, making our own way a stronger attraction than a mutual way.

In 1959, there was one divorce for about every three marriages in the United States. Sociologists say these figures do not present the entire picture of marital strain because there are untold marriages which are only "psychologically broken." They mean that such couples maintain a residence under the same roof, but man and wife are not able to come to agreement on a mutual way of life and each goes his separate way at the points where they cannot agree. The high ratio of divorce to marriage illustrates the power of the desire to turn every one to his own way.

Suppose you do communicate your true feelings, attitudes, desires? Communication, itself, will not necessarily produce unity. The desire for unity must be present. You may clarify your desires to your husband in order to get your own way. Your objective is to advance your own selfish ends, not to achieve unity. Or, as a husband, you may be firmly set against your wife's idea. Communication, then, simply clarifies the issue. It does not provide a mutual solution. Undergirding this process of communication, as Judge Hill points out, must be a firm foundation of love and unselfishness.

What of the tendency to become negative in our conversation? Bossard suggests that we heed the advice of a great teacher. He writes:

> A long time ago a great teacher pointed out that what comes out of the mouth is a great deal more important than what goes into it.[4]

This great teacher, of course, is Jesus, whom we, too, recognize for His teachings. But we go farther and acknowledge Him as our Saviour, the One who died for our sins that we might be able to walk in the newness of life. The statement Jesus made is in Matthew 15:11:

> Not that which goeth into the mouth defileth a man; but that which cometh out of the mouth, this defileth a man.

He gives further explanation in verses 18 and 19:

> But those things which proceed out of the mouth come forth from the heart; and they defile the man. For out of the heart proceed evil thoughts, murders, adulteries, fornications, thefts, false witness, blasphemies.

What is it, then, that is behind the negative conversation around the dinner table, the tendency to break fellowship by going your own way, the inclination to conceal from your most trusted companion?

It is the heart of man, which the Bible describes as "desperately wicked."

The answer, the Christian answer, to how you can maintain the kind of communication that leads to a mutual walk goes right back to your set of beliefs. Important in it is your belief in:

> The sinfulness of man.
> Redemption from sin by faith in Christ's death.
> Indwelling of the Holy Spirit which enables us to do the will of God.

---
[4]Ibid.

True Christian marriage is based on the love of God that is shed abroad in our hearts by the Holy Spirit (Rom. 5:5). That love was described in Chapter 1 as working out in our actions as part of the foundation on which the Christian marriage is based. Remember these?

Patience, kindness, generosity, humility, courtesy, unselfishness, good temper, guilelessness and sincerity.

With such love in the foundation, a Christian couple can proceed to establish and maintain a mutual way of life.

Such a foundation will enable you to approach your partner with the sincere desire to know and to be known, to listen and to share, to understand and to be understood. Thus, you are ready to build the bridge across which two-way communication can flow. Two-way communication is, first of all, a matter of the spirit. It requires two people who have been set free from the natural tendency to hide, to conceal, to be secretive. They have been set free by acknowledging that Christ died to set them free and are now submitting to the Holy Spirit, who keeps them as they continually yield to Him.

Communication is based on a combination of truth and love. Paul describes mature Christians as:

. . . no more children, tossed to and fro, and carried about with every wind of doctrine, by the sleight of men, and cunning craftiness, whereby they lie in wait to deceive; but speaking the truth in love, may grow up into him in all things, which is the head, even Christ (Eph. 4:14-15).

In the same chapter, Paul speaks of the man who is renewed in the spirit of the mind and who is created in righteousness and true holiness. To this man, Paul says:

Wherefore putting away lying, speak every man truth with his neighbor: for we are members one of another (Eph. 4:25).

We have emphasized that the natural tendency is to turn everyone to his own way. You tend to become disunited and to make judgments and decisions based on what you believe to be right and what is attractive and desirable to you. The interests of the family easily become submerged in favor of your own.

Because this is true, you must depend also on the other material besides love that goes to make up the foundation undergirding a Christian marriage—the Bible. This is the standard mutually acceptable to the serious Christian couple.

All scripture is given by inspiration of God, and is profitable for doctrine, for reproof, for correction, for instruction in righteousness: that the man of God may be perfect, throughly furnished unto all good works (II Tim 3:16, 17).

The application of this standard will, however, test the very foundation of a Christian marriage. Notice the kind of communication suggested here: Reproof, correction, instruction in righteousness. These are pointed words. Yet they reveal that the way to help maintain a "mutual" way of life is to tell your partner where he or she is wandering from your agreed-on path. This implies also your willingness to have your own wanderings pointed up.

Paul says:

Brethren, if a man be overtaken in a fault, ye which are spiritual, restore such an one in the spirit of meekness; considering thyself, lest thou also be tempted (Gal. 6:1).

Restoration—not patronizing concern for your brother (or wife), self-pity or self-seeking—is the goal.

Unacceptable or questionable behavior of others first of all should lead you to examine your own self. Perhaps if you change your way you will remove whatever has caused the other person to do as he did. Wilma did not like Fred's suggestions about the way to iron his shirts. But he continued to insist until one day she decided to do it Fred's way. His complaints turned into praise.

If after you have examined your own life and are confident before God that you are obeying Him, if you can meet the Scriptural qualification, "ye that are spiritual," then you will be on solid ground for offering a rebuke. But make sure your attitudes, feelings and thoughts about the

71

matter evidence a spirit of love. If they do not, deal with your own needs first. When you are making full use of all the Christian graces, then go to your partner.

Restoration implies reproof, correction, instruction in righteousness and recognition that adjustment has been made. This kind of communication, when done in love, leads to maintaining unity.

Restoration is a continuing process. It never ends, because we tend to go our own way. Good communications between marriage partners comes as a result of understanding this tendency toward self-will and accepting the justified reproof, correction and instruction from your partner, all undergirded by a spirit of love.

CHAPTER 6

Meeting inevitable changes

IN THIS SUSPENSE-FILLED world of ours with its dramatic changes, one fact is certain, the "certainty of uncertainty." You can expect the unexpected to happen. The mature person, especially the Christian, approaches the changes of life with interest, enjoying the variety and meeting the challenge.

Ken had been offered a college teaching job even before obtaining his bachelor's degree. This enabled him to get started in graduate school and set up a lovely apartment. Alice, his wife, became pregnant, so they happily looked forward to starting their family. The future looked good.

Some of the other men on the faculty were worried about getting drafted because they had never served in the armed forces. Ken had no such worry because he had been in the Navy during World War II. One day a letter came from the Navy notifying him that he was recalled to active duty. He was to be given an immediate overseas assignment in a remote corner of the world.

An unexpected, irreversible change had come. His wife pregnant, a career interrupted, advanced education put aside, his home disrupted. And none of the other faculty men was called.

In a matter of weeks Ken was whisked away, leaving Alice to figure out what to do with herself for two years. She tried keeping the apartment. Then she went to live with a friend. Finally, she decided to join her husband overseas. Why did this happen to them? What would this do to his education and career?

We think of the promise:

> And we know that all things work together for good to them that love God, to them who are the called according to his purpose (Rom. 8:28).

This verse seemed far-fetched to Ken and Alice—and to those who looked on. Ten years have passed. Ken's second hitch in the Navy can be viewed in the perspective of time. It turned out to be a good thing. They learned how much they appreciated one another and that they could, when necessary, live apart. They learned that seemingly insurmountable problems can be solved, that a seemingly hopeless situation will unravel. Ken has his Ph.D. degree, the kind of job he wanted, a son—and an extra maturing experience thrown in.

Why did it happen? Only God knows. But He promises:

> For I know the thoughts that I think toward you, saith the Lord, thoughts of peace, and not of evil, to give you an expected end (Jer. 29:11).

In a booklet, "Tragedy or Triumph,"[1] Dr. Donald Grey Barnhouse tells of visits to two men, each sick with tuberculosis. The first one became very angry and began to curse. "Why does God make me spit my lungs into this cup? Oh, God is so cruel to me!" He cursed God for his suffering.

[1]Barnhouse, Donald Grey, *Tragedy or Triumph*, The Bible Study Hour, 1716 Spruce St., Phila. 3, Pa., pp. 8, 9.

The second one had to spend 23 hours each day in bed and could be up for only one hour. One night he spent his hour walking and stopped in to rest where Barnhouse was preaching. He heard the story of the love of Christ and received Jesus Christ as his Saviour and Lord. From that time on, he used his daily hour to witness in the neighborhood. Soon he was too weak to go out. He asked Barnhouse to come to his home to preach to his friends. They were seated on the stairs, upstairs, in the kitchen, on the floor. After the message, this sick man said, "I know that the next time you are all together it will be for my funeral, and I want to witness to you about Christ." A few days later he died, triumphant in Christ.

Barnhouse goes on to explain:

I believe that God permits whatever happens to an unbeliever also to happen to a Christian. The unbeliever cries out against God; but the Christian says, "Lord, do to me whatever You please." No matter what your condition in life, if you are not a believer in Jesus Christ, God has a double of you somewhere who is believing in Jesus Christ. If you are in the Home for Incurables, and do not know Christ and think your lot is terrible, someone else in the Home for Incurables is praising God. The Devil has his doctors, and God has His doctors who live in simple faith and trust the Lord. The Devil has his lawyers who connive and cheat; God has His honorable, upright lawyers who seek to aid those in difficulty. God has His rich men and the Devil has his.

Describe yourself to me. Tell me how old you are, what is your education, what are your circumstances. I will duplicate them in the life of some Christian. To put it the other way around, whatever happens to a Christian, the same is happening to an unbeliever, and he is crying out, "God, you can't do this to me!" But the Christian can say, "O, God, You can do anything You wish to me. You redeemed me. You bought me with your blood. I am yours, and I know that all things will work together for good because I love You."

Peter reassures us:

Beloved, do not be surprised at the fiery ordeal coming among you to put you to the test—as though some exceptional thing were happening to you (I Pet. 4:12, Weymouth's Translation).

He says again:

These happen in order that the testing of your faith—being more precious than that of gold, which perishes but yet is proved by fire—may be found to result in praise and glory and honor at the revelation of Jesus Christ (I Pet. 1:7, Weymouth's Translation).

Change tests the mettle of the Christian, and change comes frequently to every family.

Some families have learned to anticipate change and to live with it. Others are fearful of what tomorrow may bring and their uneasiness has them so unnerved that when change comes they are floored. Still others refuse to recognize the inevitability of change and through an unnatural striving they seek to ignore it, to go on their way as if nothing had happened.

The results of that change then accumulate to the point where they fall on the family with a knock-out blow.

Think of the changes in family life since 1900. The labor-saving appliances born of electricity have revolutionized housekeeping. The automobile has moved us away from the streetcar track and into suburbia and even beyond to exurbia. Two world wars, a major depression and mounting inflation have stimulated changes in morals, customs, outlook, residence and spending. These can be called universal changes. For the most part, they have been gradual, almost creeping.

On a more personal note, families are touched by changes that affect them but not necessarily their neighbors or townspeople. A baby is born. A second one comes, bringing situations that were not known with the first one. A youngster enters school. A father is given church responsibilities that require much of his time. A teen-age son asks to use the family car for the first time.

Change came to John Simpson when it looked like the road ahead ran straight to financial success. He owned a gas station on the edge of a large city. It had taken years to build up his business so that one day when offered $100,000 for the concern he could turn it down with honest casualness. Then on another day after returning from lunch Simpson walked into the station to meet a man waiting to talk with him.

A new state highway, the man told him, was on the drawing boards. It would come right past Simpson's corner—and clip off his gas station in the process.

He would be paid according to a fair appraisal of the property. Another piece of land might even be offered in trade. But the work of years would be gone. He would no longer be on one of the best corners. He faced years of an uphill fight all over again.

John Simpson and his family experienced a change that hit deeply. So did Mike Sisco when the auto plant he had worked in 32 years closed. He was too old to get another job that amounted to much. He and his wife adjusted to the change as well as they could. They would live more simply and make their clothes and other possessions last longer. But within three weeks the neighbors, perhaps unaware of the changes that had already struck the Siscos, petitioned to have their street paved. The hard-pressed Siscos faced a payment of $400 that threw their new austerity budget off kilter.

In a brief period these changes were entered on one person's prayer card file for just three families:

Harry Thomases—Harry quitting job for another . . . necessitates family moving to neighboring state . . . Letter tells of their attending church . . . They now describe it as evangelical, not like one they attended here . . . All members of family accept Christ as Saviour.

Robert and Evelyn Brown—Long-time leaders in the church, both teaching Sunday School, singing in choir, faithful at prayer meeting, active in calling program . . . Evelyn very sick, must drop out of everything . . . Don't see much of Robert anymore. Has had to give up all but his job to care for Evelyn and the three small children.

77

Jack Wilsons—Jack has better job now . . . Family longs for TV . . . Bought it and can never pull away from it, even for Sunday night church.

Change may bring a severe test of the family's inner strengths. At such a time, how well a family has integrated its values and beliefs into its day-to-day living will be demonstrated in its ability to cope with the change.

What particular change provides the family's greatest testing? Only you can say for your family as you undergo change. Remember, gradual and expected changes may have just as great an effect over a long period as sudden and unexpected changes. Let us look briefly at both types.

Death

No change is as heart-searching as death. It causes even the most hardened to pause and examine himself. As we write this, one of our children's classmates was just recently killed in an automobile accident, a junior in high school. A man and his wife in our church were returning home from shopping last week. He slumped over the wheel and was dead at age 55. Another man, a pillar in his church, went to the doctor complaining of "the flu." He died of a heart condition in the doctor's office.

Death is to be expected. It can be sudden or with warning. Death reminds that each of us is a person and each may remain to understand what God has next for us. It will be the day-by-day faith, the values and goals which direct your life that will come into play when you are confronted with the death of someone dear to you.

Surely, the death of the father is a change that strikes a family from many directions. Cast on the wife is the burden of keeping the family together and providing a living for herself and the children. Her task will be greatly eased if they have anticipated the possibility of such a change and have planned for the continued existence of the family after his death. Life insurance is an almost universally accepted resource to hold the family together after the father's death. But preparations other than economic ought also to be

78

made. Some may be as commonplace as teaching the wife and the older children do-it-yourself jobs that usually wait on Dad's doing them.

But if money is available, most household or family business services can be purchased. What cannot be bought is the influence of a father or mother on both the remaining partner and the children to help the family continue and successfully meet its challenges even after the valued member has been taken by death.

Many are the examples of a mother's or father's prayer life and wise discipline guiding the children for years after the parent has died. Many have proved the promise in James 1:5:

> If any of you lack wisdom, let him ask of God, that giveth to all men liberally, and upbraideth not; and it shall be given him.

Death of a parent has proved to many a remaining parent that God will give you wisdom to act alone. It is God who is basically important in your life.

In some instances, death may not be the change that tugs the hardest at the family's ability to adjust. Look at some other common changes.

Sickness

Long-term illness of one member of the family will bring out whether the other members possess the spiritual fruit mentioned by Paul: Love, joy, peace, longsuffering, gentleness, goodness, faith, meekness and temperance (Gal. 5:22, 23a).

An automobile accident put a child of the Jackson family into the hospital. For months, the family made a daily trip to the hospital to visit the child. Without such visits, which were happy times for the little patient, restoration of health may never have come. A drastic change in the family schedule was necessary and it was not always easy for the visitors to make the trip or to be at the bedside the minute visiting hours began, but they did it cheerfully. Longsuffering enabled them to adjust to the change.

One of the authors remembers a family which years ago accepted the change sickness brought. The mother was frequently ill and finally the doctor sent her to bed, ordering her not to get up as long as the disease persisted. No one desired that Mother should be shut off in a bedroom away from the mainstream of family life, so her bed was moved to the living room. A bed in the living room? This family was willing to make a change that others through pride would have found impossible.

Separation

A new job in another city can bring about temporary separation. So can the frequent traveling of a father in his work. Permanent separation comes when marital conflict has led to a breakup of the home. Temporary separations may cause some new roles to be adopted or old ones shed for awhile with the willingness to go back to the former status when the separation is over. The loss of a parent from the home—through death, legal separation, or divorce—means some roles must be altered permanently and may involve not only the remaining parent but the children as well.

Economic

A pay raise can bring about change as can a reduction in income, or even loss of a job. Economic change can be up or down, gradual or sudden. The values a family holds will be important in their reaction to such change. If they live on a materialistic plane, sudden wealth can ensnare them in a ridiculous display, and their inability to handle money wisely will be readily seen by their friends and neighbors. If reverses come, they may resemble the money-hungry plungers of a generation ago who, after the financial crash of 1929, could not bear to face life in the condition of poverty in which they suddenly found themselves.

The Bible gives sound advice on reacting to economic change when Paul tells how he learned to live with the extremities of being abased and abounding and how, regardless of his state of affairs, to be content (Phil. 4:11, 12).

Bill Mays never had much of this world's goods until he married Ruth. He then coveted the help of his mother-in-law, which she generously gave, but he despised her as the giver. When he was abased he thought to abound would be happiness. When he abounded he was not able to handle himself any better. He could not see God's hand in his mother-in-law's handout.

Job changes can mean a shift in hours, upsetting established routines. Changes at the office or shop can bring a promotion that wins accolades. Or they may result in a passing over for promotion or a demotion that prompts raised eyebrows and thinly-veiled curiosity.

Economic change may mean Mother going to work, forcing her to take on the role of breadwinner and to decide how she is going to apportion her time among family, church and community.

Environment

Better or poorer housing may be in the future for your family. Or for some other reason a move to another neighborhood may be necessary. A change in neighborhoods means a change in neighbors, possibly in the school the children attend or the family church or in long-established habits of shopping or getting to work or to music lessons. The move to another state by the Harry Thomas family meant all this and more. Moving day usually is the prelude to numerous new experiences that seriously affect family life.

In an America in which environmental change seems to be the key to the day—reflecting a population explosion, the march of decadence in our cities and counteracting urban-renewal programs—in such a day, neighborhood changes can come to the family that stays put.

The cornfield-to-carport trend has put many a farm family into the heart of an urban situation. In neighborhood shifts, thousands of families have had to face up to racial issues. As the make-up of communities changes, the vague feelings on hitherto distant and impersonal problems become specific feelings. Theories must be translated into actions. As a family is swept into the changing city or mushrooming suburb, complex pressures threaten the stability of the home. More than ever, the Christian family will be driven to cling to its unchanging foundation.

Change should never be a surprise. You need not look on it as something wrong. Even creation will undergo cataclysmic changes.

> Of old hast thou laid the foundation of the earth: and the heavens are the work of thy hands. They shall perish, but thou shalt endure, yea, all of them shall wax old like a garment; as a vesture shalt thou change them, and they shall be changed (Ps. 102:25-26).
> And all the host of heaven shall be dissolved, and the heavens shall be rolled together as a scroll: and all their host shall fall down, as the leaf falleth off from the vine, and as a falling fig from the fig tree (Isa. 34:4).

The state of the believer also is to be changed. Paul wrote to the Corinthian Christians that "we shall be changed . . . this corruptible must put on incorruption, and this mortal must put on immortality" (I Cor. 15:52b-53).

But in the midst of change, we can be sure of three unchanging principles. They go back to the foundation on which the Christian home is built.

First, God does not change. The psalmist says of him, "thou shalt endure." In the next verse (27) he adds:

> But thou art the same, and thy years shall have no end.

Malachi quotes the Lord as saying, "I change not." James speaks of the Father of lights, "with whom is no variableness, neither shadow of turning." The writer to the Hebrews says, "Jesus Christ the same yesterday, and to day, and for ever."

Second, God's Word does not change. Hebrews 6:17 speaks of "the immutability of His counsel." The psalmist says:

The counsel of the Lord standeth for ever, the thoughts of his heart to all generations (Ps. 33:11).
Forever, O Lord, thy word is settled in heaven (Ps. 119:89).

And third, the state of the believer will change, but not his standing before God. In his treatise on what changes and what does not, David says of the believer:

The children of thy servants shall continue, and their seed shall be established before thee (Ps. 102:28).

The Christian, therefore, is able to look on changing circumstances through eyes that see an unchanging God. He is able to order his life according to the unchanging Word of God. He can do this and know that his future is secure because his relationship to God can never be disturbed by the forces of change.

If this is in the foundation of the Christian family, the shocks of change can be withstood, even though they reach to the very footings.

You will experience changes that call for adapting to them, but the Christian family must adapt to change within the framework of its values and beliefs. We are reminded again of what Jesus said about foundations. One house was built on a rock, the other on sand. Violent weather changes came. The house on the solid foundation stood, the other fell.

Some changes we pursue, hoping they will bring a better, more pleasant, perhaps more fruitful life. Some changes we become aware of as we grow older. This you find out when, as parents of growing children, you try to keep up with them only to discover you are not as young as you once were.

In many instances, however, it is not man's nature to desire change. Rather, we tend to be fearful of the unknown and would rather become moss covered in our old ways than risk the new. But life cannot be lived only according to what has been if life is change. Wise is the admonishment to "get on with the living."

In his pamphlet[2] Barnhouse speaks of spoiled plans. He

---

[2] *Op. cit.*, p. 11.

tells of a bird building a nest in some branches a farmer had pruned from his orchard. As the bird flew around chirping distress as if to say, "How cruel this man is," the farmer destroyed the nest. The next day the bird tried to build its nest in the pile again. And again the farmer destroyed the nest, although no doubt the bird's flutterings and scoldings meant, "This evil man. How terrible he is to destroy my nest." On the third day the farmer noticed the bird had built its nest in a rosebush near the house. He smiled and let the nest alone. The nest was completed and the eggs were laid. But before they hatched the pile of pruned branches had been burned. If the farmer had allowed the bird to build in the pile, the nest would have been destroyed. So in great kindness he had torn it apart.

Sometimes God reaches down and spoils our plans. We chirp and protest, "God, don't do this to me." But He knows what He is doing. Instead of fighting against His will, say, "Lord, show me where to build."

We ought not get distraught trying to keep one jump ahead of changes coming our way. Living in the midst of change, the Christian ought rather to commit his way to the Lord.

Trust in the Lord with all thine heart; and lean not unto thine own understanding. In all thy ways acknowledge Him, and he shall direct thy paths (Prov. 3:5, 6).

The Christian should work to acquire the ability to solve the problems that change may bring.

CHAPTER 7

Solving family problems

WE HAVE ALL heard the prayer, "Lord, help me to have the courage to change what I can change, accept what I cannot change, and the wisdom to know the difference."

You, as an ever-changing self, living with an ever-changing family, in an ever-changing world, are involved in a continuous stream of decisions to make and problems to face. Among the major decisions that set the framework for your life are these:

What vocation will I choose?

Whom shall I marry?

Where will we live?

These decisions have behind them a multitude of lesser, more routine decisions. A choice of vocation is related to many decisions that formed study habits and interests. The choice of a marriage partner is based on many decisions involving your relationships with your family, the development of your personality and the type of people with whom you choose to associate.

Other problems which will arise in your family are these:
What shall we do about TV?
How can we maintain family worship?
How can we establish a workable budget?

Although these stated problems are not dealt with in detail in this book, this chapter gives you the principles for solving the problems and making the decisions which face you and your family.

PROBLEM SOLVING

Whatever the decision to be made, the principles for making it are the same. There are seven steps:

Identify the problem.
Gather as much factual information as possible to help you select a solution.
List possible solutions.
Test each one against the facts.
Select the best one.
Put it into action.
Follow through to see if your decision has worked.

To illustrate use of these steps, consider the family which faced the decision of what to do about the dance instruction that was part of the physical education program of the school.

Identify the Problem

Should we allow our child, age 13, to take this instruction, something she wants to do?

Information toward Solution

1. The activity runs counter to our feelings about such dancing for Christians, and counter to church by-laws.

2. This activity, as we see it, places boys and girls in physical contact at an age when they are emotionally stimulated with ease and can lead to immoral conduct outside of school.

3. Not allowing her to participate can lead to:
    1) Social rejection by classmates
    2) Poor grade in physical education
    3) Hostility of teachers based on our questioning of the moral standard of their program
    4) An unhappy child
4. Assets we can think of:
    1) Outgoing personality of our daughter that has always won her friends
    2) Spiritual foundation of the home that will undergird her in any eventuality
    3) Reasonableness of most people when it comes to respecting the convictions of others
    4) Child's devotion to God

List Possible Solutions

1. Let her dance with the rest of them.
2. Ask the teacher to excuse her on the days dancing is taught so she can go to library to study.
3. Permit child to dance with girls only.
4. Try to get dance instruction stopped by making an issue of it before the school board.
5. Send her to a private school that shares our convictions.

Test Each One

By far the majority of people favor dance instruction in school, so appealing to the school board is out. To let our daughter enter in without restriction is not in line with our view of Christian conduct. To permit her to dance with girls only is to single her out for possible ridicule. This would also possibly be a first step toward unrestricted dancing. Attendance at a private school is out for financial reasons.

Select the Best One

We are left with asking the teacher to excuse our daughter from dancing and permit her to go to the library. We will rely on the teacher's co-operation, our daughter's devotion to God, her ability to make and maintain friendships, although her friends are aware of her stand.

Put It into Action

The decision was not a happy one for the child. There were tears and pleading. As best we could, we explained our reasons to her. We both went to see the teacher and principal to explain our stand.

Follow Through

We plan to visit the school in three or four weeks to see how our plan is working. We will deal with our daughter day by day as events develop.

Another family had a decision to make of a different sort. Their son, also 13, just had a close call. He was riding his bike in the street and would have been hit by a car except for the quick action of the driver. Both parents saw this happen.

The father, very angry, told the boy to put the bicycle in the garage at once and leave it there for a month. The mother disagreed, saying the punishment was too severe. Besides, this was the time to comfort the boy, not to bawl him out. The father reminded her who was boss, and the original incident touched off a heated argument about submission.

PROBLEM SOLVING ATTITUDE

These incidents point up some basic foundations that make problem solving possible.

Personal Relations

Good personal relations are necessary in order to be objective.

Approach to Problem

The problem must be approached with open-mindedness.

88

Avoid Pre-judgment

Pre-judgment should be avoided. One of the most foolish things you can do is to collect facts that support your idea and exclude anything else.

Decision Binding

The decision should be binding on all concerned and cheerfully carried out.

Know Your Responsibility

In the first instance, the parents prayerfully accumulated all the data possible, weighed all possible decisions and arrived at one they both support.

In the second incident, there was no problem solving attitude, and the incident simply exposed two parents who are far apart in their approach to problems. It seems that the one who gets most upset has his way. They have not yet settled on who takes the lead when a problem arises.

THE WILL OF GOD

Decision making, or problem solving, exposes the soul. Often there is some issue that finally sends a couple to see a counselor. They have come to a stalemate over a decision that had to be made. Questioning usually reveals that the issue is only the last of many issues that could not be resolved. Behind the inability to come to a decision lies determined selfishness rather than the desire for a mutually acceptable decision. In decision making, your values, beliefs and goals come into play. It is here that roles must be clear.

How do you discover the will of God when a decision must be made?

Authority Must Be Determined

Let every soul be subject unto the higher powers. For there is no power but of God: the powers that be are ordained of God (Rom. 13:1).

If the decision is up to you to make, then you must make

89

it as realistically as possible. The problem-solving steps will help you.

If two or more persons must arrive at a decision, the role of each person must be clear. After a careful study of the problem, a decision must be made, even though you do not both interpret the facts the same way. Responsibility for making the decision must be clear.

Attitudes Must Be Positive

The meek will he guide in judgment: and the meek will he teach his way (Ps. 25:9).

God will guide the meek, not the weak. The one who approaches a decision in a selfless way, purposed to make the best possible decision for all concerned, is the one who is able to use his judgment.

Allegiance Must Be Established

Delight thyself also in the Lord; and he shall give thee the desires of thine heart. Commit thy way unto the Lord; trust also in him and he shall bring it to pass (Ps. 37:4-5).
Commit thy works unto the Lord, and thy thoughts shall be established (Prov. 16:3).

If you understand these verses, if you seek to understand and to please God, then you can trust the desires of your heart and your thoughts, and can proceed, by faith, to exercise your judgment. It seems reasonable to add that such a person will be quite willing to weigh his desires and thoughts against all possible facts before exercising his judgment.

Values and Goals Must Be Godward

The mouth of the righteous speaketh wisdom, and his tongue talketh of judgment. The law of God is in his heart; none of his steps shall slide (Ps. 37:30-31).
The kingdom of God is not meat and drink; but righteousness, and peace, and joy in the Holy Ghost. For he that in these things serveth Christ is acceptable to God, and approved of men. Let us therefore follow after the things which

90

make for peace, and things wherewith one may edify another (Rom. 14:17-19).

The psalmist in Psalm 24 asks the question, "Who shall ascend into the hill of the Lord? or who shall stand in his holy place?" Here is a list of the characteristics of such a man:

He has clean hands,
He has a pure heart,
He has not lifted up his soul unto vanity,
He has not sworn deceitfully.

In I Thessalonians 4, Paul lists some things we ought to do if we seek the will of God:

Abstain from fornication.
Abstain from lust.
Do not defraud a brother in any matter.
Do not despise any man.
Love one another.
Study to be quiet.
Do your own business.
Work with your own hands.
Walk honestly toward those who are without.

A favorite verse is Isaiah 32:17:

The work of righteousness shall be peace; and the effect of righteousness quietness and assurance forever.

Faith Must Be Established

Who is among you that feareth the Lord, that obeyeth the voice of his servant, that walketh in darkness, and hath no light? Let him trust in the name of the Lord, and stay upon his God (Isa. 50:10).

We have given you seven steps to follow when a decision must be made. A reasonable solution to problems depends on the gathering of all the data possible that has a bearing on the decision. However, the accurate evaluation of the data depends on the character of the person who must make the decision. If more than one person is involved, the relationship between them must be a wholesome one.

In other words, decision making becomes a test of the soul, a test of relationships, a reflection of your values and goals and the way you carry out your roles.

All the paths of the Lord are mercy and truth unto such as keep his covenant and testimonies . . . His soul shall dwell at ease; and his seed shall inherit the earth (Ps. 25:10, 13).

Summary 2

This is a fascinating world. You can become absorbed in work, play, social life, family life, church activities, academic pursuits. New learning, new places, new things, new people constantly beckon. As life goes on you are forced to choose, not always between the good and the bad, but often between several challenges that are excellent. Being mindful of this, it is necessary that you consciously seek to maintain your life in a wholesome balance in the light of your Christian values and beliefs.

A successful marriage requires a husband and wife to fit their roles together so they may be united and walk a mutual pathway. To achieve a relationship of understanding, openness and good fellowship there must be a continuous process of sharing feelings and viewpoints. Both praise and rebuke are involved. The natural tendency is to conceal, to go your own way. Only by drawing on the love of God and making the Bible the standard can communication be maintained that keeps open the mutual pathway.

Changes will come. They may involve the family in death, sickness, economic betterment or reverses, environmental changes. But the Christian has a sure foundation—faith in an unchanging God and His changeless counsel. Such a position enables him to meet changes with confidence and, committing his way to the Lord, to solve the problems that change brings.

The first section has considered the fact that what you are as a person is of utmost importance. In the second, you have learned something of the mutuality that you must achieve with your partner if your marriage is to be a stable, serene, successful relationship. Now we are ready to turn to the relationships between parents and their children—the meaning of growing with your children, the matter of discipline, the teaching about sex and the preparation of teen-agers for homes of their own.

CHAPTER 8

Growing with your children

LAUNCHING AND COMPLETING a marriage can be compared to launching and completing a college education.

John, a high school senior, is a brilliant student: mostly A's; a fine athlete; a four-letter man; popular socially; president of his class and well liked; from a happy Christian home; busy at his church—an officer and active in his youth group. We can confidently say that John has a fine background for success in college.

Even so, when he goes to college, John at best will be an outstanding freshman. We would not expect him to possess the knowledge, the experience, the maturity, the judgment or the social graces of the college senior. Such qualities are the result of four years of class attendance, study, practice, contact with others, effort, persistence, choices that contribute to his development. Becoming a successful, well-adjusted college senior is a four-year process, even for the most talented freshman.

In the women's section of our local newspaper today appeared a write-up on the wedding of two popular young people. Janet and Jim, the couple, have started out on their marriage. Each brings a particular background to it. Like John, who is an outstanding freshman, this couple, although outstanding in qualifications, are at best just beginners at the task of marriage. We do not expect them to possess the wisdom of seasoned veterans who have raised a fine family and who now look on as their children establish their own homes.

STAGES IN FAMILY DEVELOPMENT

Marriage, like a college education, is a process. It requires years of study, effort, persistence, choices that contribute to the wholesome development of the marriage.

David B. Treat, director of the Clara Elizabeth Fund for Maternal Health in Flint, Michigan, one of the nation's most comprehensive family-life programs, uses a chart to

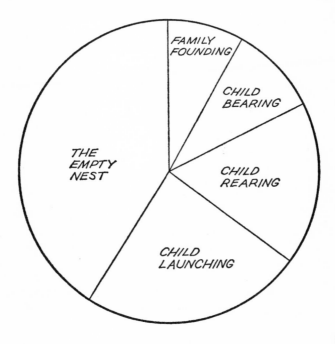

show some of the stages that a typical marriage passes through. The chart is cut up like a pie, showing the average amount of time each stage occupies in the marriage cycle.

It is difficult to describe any one marriage in terms of a cycle. Each of the stages may be longer or shorter than the average. Some families are in several stages at one time. Some marriages are interrupted by divorce or death. But the chart does show clearly that most marriages pass through a series of stages that are well defined and can be anticipated and prepared for.

Glick has produced a timetable that gives a good visual picture of the family's life cycle, based on statistics brought out in the 1950 census:[1]

Stages of the Life Cycle of the Family	Median Age of the Husband	Median Age of the Wife
A. First Marriage	22.8	20.1
B. Birth of First Child[2]	25.2	22.5
C. Birth of Last Child	28.8	26.1
D. Marriage of Last Child	50.3	47.6
E. Death of One Spouse	64.1	61.4
F. Death of Other Spouse	71.6	77.2

A study of the chart and timetable shows that the average family has a very brief period—two years or less—before the childbearing stage begins. In other words, marriage usually implies parenthood. Parenthood implies the responsibility for the training of children.

PANORAMA OF THE CHILD'S GROWTH

It is a paradox, but seemingly true, that a helpless infant rules the household. The baby is dependent on his parents for all his needs—feeding, bathing, changing and, often, get-

[1] Adapted from Glick, Paul C., "The Life Cycle of the Family," *Marriage and Family Living*, Vol. XVII, No. 1, February, 1955, p. 4.

[2] Figures for Birth of First Child are based on Vital Statistics, not the census and Glick does not include them in his chart.

ting off to sleep—and at least a good deal of family activity revolves around these. As the infant grows older, he learns to hold his bottle, play with a toy and amuse himself and in general to fit himself into a schedule that is less exacting on other members of the family.

By the time he is a year old, he may be able to walk. He has learned simple tricks to get what he wants. Mealtime finds him trying to feed himself, although he is still dependent on others for any serious feeding.

Little by little he learns words that meet his needs, and he becomes adept at doing things for himself. By the time he is ready for school, he has become a personality to be reckoned with, not only in the family, but with his playmates and the family's circle of friends.

In his younger school years, he sometimes ventures out of the shelter of family understanding, but is only too glad to scurry back into it when he discovers that the sun does not rise and set solely on him. He comes to know a good deal about responsibility and privilege and, in the Christian home, he realizes that man, including himself, is accountable to God. He acquires many motor and manual skills, like bike riding and use of simple tools. Bravery, loyalty, imagination blossom in this period. Sex differences become manifest in attitudes and interests.

As the boy progresses in the teens, he is perplexed by many things—perhaps because he is on the threshhold of an adult world, but not quite in it. Inner conflicts come when he finds his early training put to severe tests by a world he before hardly knew existed. At first he is fiercely loyal to his own sex, then opens his life to include those of the other sex. He exhibits an outward passion to conformity and is addicted to fads. Physically, his strength and stamina may not be able to keep up with his rapid growth. Personal appearance becomes important. He handles his own money, buys most of his own clothes, works at a variety of jobs and is beginning to think seriously of a career. At times he becomes almost a child again, as if he is afraid or reluctant to grow up, but by and large he is arriving at adulthood.

One of the most useful helps to the student of family living is the concept of the "developmental task." Havighurst[3] describes the tasks a person must learn—the developmental tasks of life—as

> those things which constitute healthy and satisfactory growth in our society. They are the things a person must learn if he is to be judged and to judge himself to be a reasonably happy and successful person. *A developmental task is a task which arises at or about a certain period in the life of an individual, successful achievement of which leads to his happiness and to success with later tasks, while failure leads to unhappiness in the individual, disapproval by the society and difficulty with later tasks.*

Consider the task of learning to talk, Havighurst explains,

> Sometime between the ages of one and two most children master the essentials of human speech and language . . . If the task is not learned, the failure will stand in the way of learning a series of later tasks, which depend greatly upon language.

There are two reasons why this concept is helpful to educators, he says. And if we can transfer his reasoning from the school to the home, it first of all helps the parents to discover the nature of the job confronting them. Second, it helps give some idea of the timing of the parents' efforts. It helps discover when conditions are most favorable for learning these tasks, which Havighurst calls "the teachable moment."

> When the body is ripe, and society requires, and the self is ready to achieve a certain task, the teachable moment has come.

Briefly stated are a series of developmental tasks at various age-levels adapted from Havighurst:

Infancy and early childhood

1. Learning to walk.

[3] Havighurst, Robert J., *Developmental Tasks and Education*, Longman, Green and Co., New York, 1952.

2. Learning to take solid foods.
3. Learning to talk.
4. Learning to control the elimination of body wastes.
5. Learning sex differences and sexual modesty.
6. Achieving physiological stability.
7. Forming simple concepts of social and physical reality.
8. Learning to relate one's self emotionally to parents, siblings and other people.
9. Learning to distinguish right from wrong and developing a conscience.

Middle childhood (age 6 to 12)

1. Learning physical skills necessary for ordinary games.
2. Building wholesome attitudes toward one's self as a growing organism.
3. Learning to get along with others of own age.
4. Learning to behave like boys or girls.
5. Developing fundamental skills in reading, writing and calculating.
6. Developing concepts necessary for everyday living.
7. Developing the conscience, morality and a scale of values.

Adolescence (age 12 to 18)

1. Accepting one's body and a masculine or feminine role.
2. Developing new relationships with others of same age of both sexes.
3. Becoming emotionally independent of parents and other adults.
4. Achieving assurance of economic independence.
5. Selecting and preparing for an occupation.
6. Developing concepts and intellectual skills necessary for civic and social duty.
7. Desiring and achieving socially responsible behavior.
8. Preparing for marriage and family life.

Early adulthood (age 18 to 30)

1. Selecting a mate.

2. Learning to live with a marriage partner.
3. Starting a family.
4. Rearing children.
5. Managing a home.
6. Getting started in an occupation.
7. Taking on civic responsibility.
8. Finding a congenial social group.

Middle age (age 30 to about 55)

1. Achieving adult civic and social responsibility.
2. Establishing and maintaining an economic standard of living.
3. Assisting teen-age children to become responsible and happy adults.
4. Developing adult leisure activities.
5. Falling back on the couple's role after the nest is empty.
6. Accepting and adjusting to physiological changes of middle age.
7. Adjusting to aging parents.

Later maturity

1. Adjusting to decreasing physical strength and health.
2. Adjusting to retirement and reduced income.
3. Adjusting to death of spouse.
4. Becoming an active member of one's own age group.
5. Establishing satisfactory living arrangements.

THE CHALLENGE

We have included the stages of marriage and a list of developmental tasks in order to give you a panoramic view of the task of parenthood. This is an everchanging task. The child is not the only one who is growing. You grow along with him.

Growing with the first child can be likened to the school teacher who is presenting a particular course for the first time. Most likely, he can keep just one step ahead of his class and in the presentation of his material he never knows whether it will be effective until he tries it out on the class.

Teaching that same course the second year is much easier—and better for the new class. He knows his material more intimately, has added to it from new sources and as he is more confident, spends less time in preparing. But he also has other courses to teach, possibly a new one requiring development of a new set of notes and teaching outline. Thus, the job always gets bigger and more complicated.

It is the same with the parent. You can expect to be better informed and better prepared to guide each child as he comes along. Dealing with the second child will be more "routine" than it was with the first. Things that bothered you with the first will be "old stuff" with those that come after. But there will be the complication of being a parent to children of different age levels, each presenting a "teachable moment," often simultaneously, on widely differing developmental tasks.

Parenthood requires that mothers and fathers grow along with their children, that they understand the stages and study each child and that they guide the development program of each child step by step.

One of the authors is the father of five children. He is familiar with the mass production of automobiles in the highly mechanized factories of his home town, and also with a small shop turning out fine furniture in a nearby village. A recent trip to the furniture shop reminded him of rearing children. In the size of his family, he concedes, his case may be more like the mass production of the automobile. But the process of raising it is like the craftsman's furniture making. Each of the products is custom built and requires his patient shaping, sanding, fitting, molding and polishing.

Do not make the mistake of thinking that the stages of development are steady and that progress is of a constantly accelerating speed. If you keep this in mind you will not become discouraged when you think your child is making no headway in a given task. Rather, you will learn patience and will know that what seems to be a marking of time will someday give way to a learning of double-time cadence.

The writer of Ecclesiastes puts it this way:

To every thing there is a season, and a time to every purpose under the heaven: A time to be born, and a time to die; a time to plant, and a time to pluck up that which is planted (Eccles. 3:1, 2).

Isaiah asks a question and then answers it:

Whom shall he teach knowledge? and whom shall he make to understand doctrine? them that are weaned from the milk, and drawn from the breasts. For precept must be upon precept, precept upon precept; line upon line, line upon line; here a little, and there a little (Isa. 28:9, 10).

The parent must develop skill in identifying the teachable moment, that fleeting period of time when the child is ready to learn a task that must be taught.

As in any profession, parental study, effort, and growth never end. Changing circumstances continuously offer new challenges. As in any profession also, the best qualified parent seeks help through constant reading, organized classes, government and private agencies. Here the church has a golden opportunity to offer the help that parents need for their task within a Christian setting.

Anna Wolf[4] has written a book in which she gives her views on methods of childrearing. Her conclusion, however, points to the character of the parent:

In the end, parents will teach with their lives, not with their words; with what they are, not with procedures and methods. Growing up in a home where two adults have lived together lovingly, loyally and responsibly teaches more than any other experience or any special methods can possibly teach.
Parents, then, must put their own house in order as best they can and must be willing, if they feel in danger of failing, to seek help for themselves as well as for their children. Their way of working out their problems as adults, the manner and direction of their own loving and hating will, when all is said and done, be the paramount facts in their child's emotional development and happiness.

The Christian parent has ample resource to assure him of doing an adequate job.

---

[4] Wolf, Anna W. M., *The Parents' Manual*, Simon and Schuster, New York, 1947, p. 184.

CHAPTER 9

Facing child discipline

PEOPLE APPROACH parenthood in two ways. Some seek to teach children what is right by punishing them when they do wrong. Others teach what is right by keeping the child in the paths of righteousness.

These two ways are represented by two common questions.

The first: "How should I discipline (or punish) my child when he misbehaves?" The thought behind the question is that a child should be made to suffer if he misbehaves.

To illustrate this approach, one parent wanted to teach her child not to spill her milk. Her approach was this: "If you spill your milk I will spank you."

She looked on as the child proceeded to spill her milk and then spanked her. This process was repeated for many weeks. The pattern of teaching between this mother and child became, "If you do it, or refuse to do it, I will hit you."

The second question: "How can I discipline (or guide) my child into paths of righteousness?"

Another parent wanted to teach her child not to spill her milk. She watched closely, teaching the child to put the glass down far enough out of range so that random movements would not spill the milk.

"Put the glass over here so you won't spill your milk." When the child forgot, her mother reminded her. At times, the child chose to defy her mother and deliberately sought to spill the milk. The mother, moving quickly, simply prevented the child from doing it. Sometimes she spanked the child's hand to teach her that she would not be allowed to spill it. The pattern of teaching between mother and child became, "This is what we do. I will see that you do it."

Both parents had to deal with defiance. Both sought to accomplish the same thing. However, there were two distinct approaches. In one case, allowing a child to disobey and then punishing her; in the other, teaching a child what to do and using whatever means necessary to see that the child did it.

We believe this second purpose more nearly fulfills the familiar Bible verse:

> Train up a child in the way he should go: and when he is old, he will not depart from it (Prov. 22:6).

What Is Discipline?

We think of a disciplined person as one who has chosen a certain way of life and voluntarily continues in his chosen way. To "discipline" a child is not to punish him for stepping out of line, but is to proceed to teach that child the way he ought to go. This includes everything that you do in order to help children learn. The parent does his part along with the school, church, other agencies and society in general. Discipline involves a twenty-year process. During this time you slowly relinquish complete control in favor of the gradually developing inner strengths of the child that enable him to take responsibility for his own conduct and its consequences.

Discipline involves teaching the child to accept activities that are not open to debate, like necessary routines at home, in school, church and community. It involves teaching standards by which the child can judge his own behavior. It also involves teaching him to face the problems of life with confidence, hope, eagerness, determination. The disciplined person adds daily to his fund of knowledge, his relationships bring more satisfaction than annoyance, his attitude toward life is one of courage. He has a zest for living. If your child grows up to take upon himself this kind of life, your training of him has been good.

In the meantime, you must use all the skill, knowledge and help available to interpret and to teach your values to your children. If you can do this and enjoy the process through each swiftly passing phase, then the "discipline problem" will become a pleasant task, not something to make you cringe—the task of leading your children to an abundant life.

The Foundation for Discipline

All forms of discipline, to be successful, must be based on the foundation of love. The understanding that many people have of the place of love in guidance of their children is reflected in such questions as:

"Should I withdraw my love when I punish my child?"

"Should I show that I love him after I punish him?"

Parents asking these questions usually are thinking in terms of giving or withholding hugs and kisses. The foundation that we speak of is a matter of the spirit, not something that you do. We refer to the "spectrum of love." As one man put it, "I kiss my wife good-by, but her lips are hard." They steadfastly keep up the motions of expressing affection, but the spirit is wrong. The same holds true in dealing with children. Love is not something that you do; it is something that is in you. Your love ought to be constant, not related to your child's behavior. In love you help your child to repeat acceptable behavior and in love you restrain him, if necessary, from repeating unacceptable behavior.

It is said of God that He chastens whom He *loves*. Further,

> Now no chastening for the present seemeth to be joyous, but grievous: nevertheless afterward it yieldeth the peaceable fruit of righteousness unto them which are exercised thereby (Heb. 12:11).

Chastening, or correcting, is not a happy experience for the child, but in love you look beyond the present. Your task is to help him become a mature, responsible adult, not to keep him smiling today at any price.

Praise for a job well done reassures a child. Admonition for a job poorly done lets him know he is not learning well. Neither praise nor admonition is evidence of love, however.

You can praise someone for having performed a beautiful solo and at the same time be filled with jealousy or animosity toward that person. A home where everyone gets a welcoming kiss and plenty of praise can still be a cold place. A warm, loving, friendly home is a matter of the spirit.

There are many styles of managing a home. Some are strict, some are lenient. It is not the style that makes the difference, but the spirit.

Every family faces the same basic challenges. Among family members are differences in age, personality, interest, needs and capacities. We all know families who manage to operate smoothly. In love, the parents make it their business to be sensitive to the needs of each member and meet them without injuring any other member.

The Major Task

For the Christian, the major task is to teach your children from the beginning that you are followers of the Master, that your children need Christ as Saviour, that they should keep God central in their lives, that you look for the return of Christ.

Mark Fakkema, has written a pamphlet titled, "How to Teach Obedience."[1] He makes these three points:

[1]Fakkema, Mark, *How To Teach Obedience*, National Association of Christian Schools, 10201 S. State St., Chicago, Ill.

1. Begin as early as possible to teach your child to fear God. If we truly fear God we are ready to follow His command to teach His will diligently to our children when we sit in our houses, when we walk by the way and when we lie down and when we rise (Deut. 6:6, 7). Since "by him were all things created . . . and by him all things consist" (Col. 1:16, 17), it is clear that parents have ample occasion to inspire awesome reverence for Him who alone is worthy of all love and all-out devotion.

2. Begin as early as possible to teach your children respect for God-given authority. Since there is no power but of God (Rom. 13:1), parents who exercise authority must do so under God's orders, in God's name and in the greatness, the power, the majesty, the glory, the righteousness and the justice, grace and love of God.

3. Be sure that your commands to your children are expressive of God's will. It should ever be apparent that your commands are God-inspired. To teach God's will without knowing the Bible is to teach your own will—and to fail in the teaching of obedience.

These are thoughtful words. The practice of them will require many years of diligent effort and study. Paul, the apostle, sums it up this way:

> And, ye fathers, provoke not your children to wrath: but bring them up in the nurture and admonition of the Lord (Eph. 6:4).

Parenthood, then, brings you back to a consideration of your values.

In one family the parents were having great difficulty with a daughter in her late teens. She was rude in her speech, refused to carry out routines, challenged their authority. This situation led the parents to some careful heart searching. They came to the conclusion that they had not been thinking of themselves as being responsible to God as parents, nor as being responsible for teaching His will to their children. They had a talk with their daughter. On the strength of the Word of God, they pointed out that He required her obedience and that He required them to bring her up in the nurture and admonition of the Lord. Neither parents nor child had the power to alter these facts.

Through study of His Word, parents and child received a new slant on their responsibilities. There have been relapses, but basically they now live happily together as each seeks to be obedient to God.

Discipline Involves Knowledge

Guiding children implies a purpose and a goal. It suggests that parents assume responsibility for influencing their children and making learning wholesome and effective.

This responsibility includes the necessity to comprehend the needs of children and to understand how youngsters develop and their processes of learning. Your desire to learn about your task and your willingness to risk making mistakes will enable you to study and practice the procedures successfully used by other adults.

As you put your ideas into practice, you will gradually acquire more and more skill in the art of arranging experiences that foster wholesome, happy development. You will thereby develop understanding and, in time, conviction. The effectiveness of any procedure is limited by the confidence of the adult that he can use it for the child's good. Confidence and conviction will dissipate the fear of breeding hostilities that can misdirect the child throughout life.

Children who live in an atmosphere of loving effort can survive many technical mistakes. Parenthood is a matter of feelings, enjoyment, dedication, more than techniques.

A mother asked for help because her ten-year-old was a feeding problem. Questioning revealed that the child came home from school and had unlimited sandwiches, cookies and fruit before supper. It was suggested that she eliminate any eating between meals. The mother was amazed at my suggestion. To her, this would be cruelty. She could still remember how she felt when her mother refused her food. She had tried this and her child cried bitterly. Nevertheless, the fact that the child merely picked at her supper was a source of irritation to both parents. The child was careless about family routines, which also greatly annoyed her mother. Over a period of time, she came to realize that her own response to her child fell far short of the "spectrum of love." Parenthood, to her, was a bothersome task.

As she saw her own need, she turned to God for His love. After much reassurance, she became bold enough to refuse her child food between meals and insisted that she observe family routines. At times, she resorted to spankings and keeping the child from meeting her friends until her room was cleaned up.

Slowly, the child's resistance yielded under her mother's now friendly, firm supervision. Gradually, the mother grew in understanding of her responsibility and it became a sure conviction. Her success with her child was in proportion to her own development.

Discipline Requires Adult Conviction

Uncertainty on the part of an adult about the direction that guidance should take indicates a lack of proper study and consideration. A sure sense of direction—so sure that the adult conveys it to the child in word and deed—is essential to effective guidance. Look at the Biblical view:

> The rod and reproof give wisdom: but a child left to himself bringeth his mother to shame (Prov. 29:15).

> Correct thy son, and he shall give thee rest. Yea, he shall give delight to thy soul (Prov. 29:17).

> As many as I love, I rebuke and chasten: be zealous therefore, and repent (Rev. 3:19).

Adults who leave the child's achievements at the level of getting their own way and their development within the limits of their interest of the moment are not guiding. Such adult action—or inaction—is irresponsibility, not guidance.

A child has the right to expect that his parents know better than he and that they lead the way. He should be able to expect them to possess a conviction strong enough to carry him along, at times against his resistance or inertia. The decision on how to best satisfy the fundamental needs of a child rests not on the inexperience and inclination of a child, but on the parents' knowledge of the child's needs.

Just because a child cries for a candy bar, refuses milk, resists sleep, insists on darting across the street, it does not follow that he knows better than the adults in his life what is good for him.

The Moyers had the problem of dealing with a teen-age son who would not go to bed when told. Because of his late hours, his school work suffered and eventually he contracted tuberculosis. An important cause, the doctor reported, was fatigue. This boy's parents had failed him. What will make a child thrive physically and socially is an adult decision which is gradually given over to the child as he shows himself capable of handling decisions effectively. There is no magic formula on procedure. What you do and the way you do it is a compound of your knowledge, your values and your inner strengths.

Discipline Involves Supervision

One mother tacked a sheet of paper on the wall and said sweetly to her three-year-old: "This part of the wall is for you." She had read somewhere that this was the way to do it. She returned in a half hour and to her dismay found Ricky had torn down the paper and very seriously and busily was covering the wall with a preschooler's design. She learned a lesson at the expense of a new wallpapering job. What was the lesson? You cannot expect too much obedience from a small child without supervision.

Reasoning is not effective as a substitute for supervision. Another mother learned this. As she tenderly put a coat on her six-year-old Ruthie, she explained carefully that the spring air was very crisp and this coat would give just the warmth to prevent a cold. Ruthie apparently accepted this explanation and Mother went about her work happily. An hour later she caught a glimpse of Ruthie playing in a flimsy blouse. The coat was on the grass, soaking up the spring dampness. Ruthie had not absorbed her mother's concern over her health. It simply got too hot with the coat on. The result? A cold that lasted for days.

Whose responsibility was it? The child disobeyed. But she thought getting too warm was cause enough for a change in Mother's orders. Her mother learned she could not rely on reasoning about health over comfort with a six-year-old. Supervision was required.

Discipline Involves Limits

Some boundaries are necessary for the well-being of each child, and to guide two or more people in living together harmoniously. We will call these "limits."

Specific limits ought to be as few as possible, reasonable, enforceable, withdrawn (or modified as the child grows older). Illustrations in this chapter refer to limits involving feeding, adequate sleep, respect for property, adequate clothing, respect for the comfort of others.

Privileges should be deserved before being granted and should be withdrawn if the accompanying responsibilities are not fulfilled. For example, two girl friends, both 14, like to alternate week ends at each other's houses. This privilege is based on homework being done as well as chores around the house.

If a privilege is no longer deserved, or if a request cannot be granted, the decision should be made promptly and forthrightly. A child of any age can accept a negative answer much easier than a postponed answer. A decision, once made with consideration given to both the child's and the adult's point of view, should not be reversed unless some new facts are introduced.

Teen-agers are inclined to regard certain privileges as their rights, like use of the car, choice of clothing, the hour to get home and to bed. It is up to the parent to have a clear understanding with the child about the use of the car, buying of clothing, hours. Any failure to observe the limits should involve automatic curtailment of the privilege involved.

111

Parents should carefully avoid threats of punishment that cannot be enforced. Certainty of punishment is more important than the nature of the punishment. Empty threats encourage disrespect for the parents and for all authority.

Discipline Involves Help[2]

Parents give help to their youngsters as a part of the thrust into life. The child is guided into discovering his own abilities and this guidance continues as he develops them until he becomes independent in his effective use of them. How can you help? He may need physical help for what he cannot do. He may need explanation or demonstration for what he does not know or understand. Or he may need encouragement, even insistence, for what he does not want to do or lacks confidence to try.

Before undertaking to influence a child you yourself must be sure of what you expect of him. You must be sure that what you expect is within his ability. And you must be satisfied that it is worthy of both his effort and yours. Whether the experience you plan for the child measures up can be learned by applying three tests:

> Will he find frequent use at his age and in his environment for the behavior I am trying to help him learn?
> Will he continue to find it useful as he grows older?
> Will it lead to other useful behavior?

When you have decided that the goal you have selected for your child is worthy, another decision confronts you: Is this the proper time for him to attempt it, or would he learn with less strain and more profit at a later time? These questions will help you decide:

> Is it simple and definite enough for him to know what is expected of him?
> Is it easy enough for him to learn without strain?
> Is it interesting enough for him to find satisfaction in it as he gains skill?

Most children, when they find the goal a worthy one and

---

[2] The material in this section is adapted from "Principles for Child Guidance," Cornell Extension Bull. 420, by Ethel B. Waring, Cornell Univ., Ithaca, N. Y., 1952.

the undertaking within their abilities, will soon take over the parent's goal as their own and as they progress in achievement will require less and less help or encouragement from anyone.

A child may be guided indirectly or directly. Waring lists these examples of indirect guidance:

Change the time or place for some of his behavior. (Give him his bath before supper so he can have a quiet story before he goes to bed.)

Provide him with more or better equipment, supplies and resources. (Fix low hooks for his clothes.)

Plan situations in which he will be likely to choose, prepare and plan; take responsibility; or act in any other desired way. (While he is napping, set up his easel with two colors of paint.)

She lists these as direct methods of guidance:

Encourage his effort and approve his behavior. (When his wagon wheel gets stuck, you might say, "Good, you are lifting it out.")

Give physical aid. (Push a little as he pulls.)

Help Involves Pressure

Guiding children involves dealing with resistance.

There are times when the natural inclination of a child is not in his best interests. There are benefits to him that you see which the child cannot see.

For example, a father knew that his teen-age daughters wanted to learn water skiing. They were afraid to try. Knowing his daughters, he believed them perfectly capable of learning this skill. He insisted that they try and within an hour both were happily enjoying the sport.

Another child insisted on playing around deep water. He could not understand the danger. His mother scooped him up, kicking and screaming, and put him behind a fence where he would be safe. Ignoring his screaming, she confidently redirected his activity by getting him started playing with a toy truck.

This is pressure; it may be as strong or gentle as necessary.

In a restaurant recently, a preschool child was holding the door open, allowing a chilling blast of cold air to come in. The waitress talked to the boy to no avail. The mother said, "Darling, everyone is getting cold. Please close the door." He refused. The mother was helpless. A man sitting near by decided he could help, so he walked up to the boy, took hold of his arm and marched him to his mother, saying firmly, "Leave the door closed." The mother looked at the man admiringly and asked, "How did you do it? He won't listen to me." The boy needed the guidance of an adult who felt strongly that it was a reasonable request that the door be closed. The child kept eyeing the man, but stayed in his seat.

Pressure is everything outside the individual that influences or directs him in what he does, thinks or feels. This is a constructive force that slowly leads him to satisfactions he would not otherwise discover and to develop abilities he did not know he had. Pressure leads him to a knowledge of right and wrong.

Admittedly such guidance is a force, enough to overcome the child's resistance. The stronger the force, the greater is the danger of misuse, whether the misuse is deliberate or with the best of intent.

Many persons fear to use pressure, which prevents their using it effectively. Some parents feel this will incite hostility. Others fear social disapproval, that they will be thought of as harsh parents or teachers. Still others fear their own incompetence, their inability to carry through to success.

It is obvious that pressure can be misused. It can become coercion for selfish gain. The parent may have his own comfort in mind or his own needs, not the common good of the family. Such coercion does incite hostility. It dwarfs a child's development, never leaving him free to act or learn. To the extent that it is not resisted, it will make the child dependent for he has scant opportunity to achieve on his own and to make decisions from which he can learn.

Coercion used by the adult for personal gain is not guidance as we use the term—defined as the effort of the adult to influence the child toward experiences, which in his judgment will be for the child's development. This definition places squarely on the adult the responsibility to decide what is of value to the child.

Dealing with resistance requires firm convictions that can withstand a child's temporary opposition and at times public condemnation. Essential are an understanding of the child's needs and pattern of development and ways of helping the child. You need faith to test your learnings and with each test to strengthen your conviction or modify it in some way. Conviction based on continuous testing of your belief by faith displaces both dependence on approval and fear of disapproval. An adult who cannot trust himself to decide what is good for his child starts off with a handicap, for he lacks focus and precision in his effort. No guidance procedure will help him, no matter how successful it may be for another understanding, skillful and confident adult. A very young child with determined purpose can prevent such an adult from making good on any attempt to direct him. Such parents say, "But he won't." "I can't make him."

Deep conviction on the part of the adult, reinforced by the parents' own example, is basic to guidance. For example, the roots of real courtesy are not just in saying "please" and "thank you," but in the feeling of courtesy, in genuine interest and kindliness. In the same way, real ambition, independence, unselfishness, honesty and integrity develop from within. You can help by creating an atmosphere where these things are present.

Resisting of adult authority is to be expected from children. Paul quoted the psalmist:

As it is written, There is none righteous, no, not one (Rom. 3:10).

This natural tendency is faced by all parents. Resistance is a means of control that many children are allowed to use, day in and day out. Some carry this spirit into adulthood without having been taught its true nature and the remedy.

In our experience, children are not at ease when they are "getting away with something." Even a rebellious child is bewildered and disturbed by a parent who indulges his lawlessness, even though he makes it as hard for the parent as possible. Children feel better when definite standards are set up. These are safeguards if they are administered firmly and with kindness.

This leads us to something not often thought of as related to discipline—family worship.

Family Devotions

This is a time when the family pauses and together worships the Lord. Everywhere we hear that the key to family success is this period that we call the "family altar." This practice should be carried out steadily and persistently like attendance at school and consistent medical and dental care.

It can be a time when members of the family share questions, doubts, thoughts, problems and answers. It can be a time of true "togetherness." It can be a time of hearing one another pray, learning verses of Scripture together—which makes such learning easier and more fun—helping children apply the teaching of the Word to their school subjects.

In our experience, however, parents speak of the maintenance of the family altar as a difficult task. The children sometimes resist it. It is difficult to keep interesting. Parents are forever looking for some book or other aid that will make it more attractive.

The success of the family altar, in our opinion, is a matter of *conviction* more than a matter of technique or carefully chosen material. The basic question is: Is it vital to the welfare of your child?

It is normal for you to see that your child does what you consider important to him. When supper is ready you round up the family regardless of whether they are absorbed in something else. There is no question about your child going to school. If he has trouble with his studies it never occurs to you to let him stay home from classes for a while.

You take him to the doctor or dentist even if he screams and you must hold him down. You do not think yourself to be unreasonable or mean. You do not wonder if he will rebel against education or medical or dental care when he is older. You know that as he grows up he will see the need for continuing these practices.

As you consider the family altar vital to the child's and your welfare, you will see that it is carried out. You will overlook resistance to it as you do in other matters.

Bible reading, the use of devotional books and aids will be successful only as you consistently carry out this practice with the conviction that it is of vital benefit. And it goes without saying that the benefit of the family altar should be reflected in the relationship of husband and wife and in their spirit toward the children and others. If this is so, you can be assured that your child will not discard a practice or a faith that he finds beneficial to him.

CHAPTER 10

Communicating sex education

THERE ARE APPROXIMATELY as many men as there are women in the world. They encounter each other in the neighborhood, at church and school; as bank tellers, gasoline station attendants, salesmen, grocerymen, stenographers; as relatives; as marriage partners. Sex education, properly taught, will prepare boys and girls for mature relationships in adolescence and adulthood. Sex education, as we see it, includes everything that has to do with the differences in body and behavior between men and women.

What is man? The first chapter of the Bible has this to say about him:

So God created man in his own image, in the image of God created he him; male and female created he them. And God blessed them, and God said unto them, Be fruitful, and multiply, and replenish the earth, and subdue it . . . (Gen. 1:27, 28).

And God saw everything that he had made, and, behold, it was very good . . . (Gen. 1:31a).

The human body is one of the greatest miracles in the universe. It is a creation of God. It is God who made us male and female. One of the greatest wonders of all is that the Creator would entrust us with the power to pass life on to someone else and add to this the responsibility of training and raising the new life. It is God who gave His blessing to Christian marriage as the plan for fellowship between man and woman and as the means of replenishing the earth.

In writing to the Corinthians Paul gave this wise counsel:

Let the husband render unto the wife due benevolence; and likewise also the wife unto the husband. The wife hath not power of her own body, but the husband: and likewise also the husband hath not power of his own body, but the wife. Defraud ye not one the other, except it be with consent for a time, that ye may give yourselves to fasting and prayer; and come together again, that Satan tempt you not for your incontinency (I Cor. 7:3-5).

Benevolence carries the meaning of good will and kindness in the thoughts and feelings toward your partner. The spirit of this passage gives great importance to the sexual relationship in combination with "due benevolence." It is evil to deprive your partner, except it be with consent. You will note that the only basis for depriving one another is for the purpose of fasting and prayer. It is significant that benevolence, the sexual relationship, fasting and prayer are mentioned together. All of these are holy, proper and necessary activities.

In my experience in marriage counseling, I find some strain over the sexual relationship present in almost every couple which comes for help. A lack of due benevolence and mutual consideration is also involved. When a couple begins to correct the matter of mutual benevolence in marriage, the sexual problem will usually clear up.

Your attitude toward each other and your treatment of each other as a married couple will have an important part in the sex education of your children. The way you think and behave will go a long way in determining how your son or daughter will react to a person of the opposite sex.

You will bring to your marriage attitudes and feelings about your body that previous experience has taught you. These may or may not correspond to the attitudes and feelings that your partner brings. If you will exercise due benevolence one toward another, you will achieve a mutually satisfactory relationship one toward another.

David B. Treat says sex education is 20 per cent education and 80 per cent attitudes. Tender, considerate, unselfish, kind, mutual consideration for one another in the family will contribute to developing right attitudes in the child toward the opposite sex. The child must see a display of affection in the home—not merely hugs and kisses, but mutual consideration in a loving spirit.

Dr. Paul Popenoe, a noted authority on marriage, writes:

> The finding of love is not a destination—it is a journey; a creative experience in which a man and a woman accept the full responsibilities of adults in a partnership through which each gives everything as well as receives everything. Sex is built into this partnership as one of the foundation stones, along with tenderness, affection, esteem, intellectual companionship, economic interests and the creation of a home and children. These diverse elements have to be brought together and kept together; they have to be lived together. The combination has so much to offer, so much to contribute to life, that no one can afford to miss it.[1]

We have said that your body is a creation of God. He designed it, including the reproductive system. He did not create a good part and a bad part, a clean side and a dirty side. He created it all and called it very good. Therefore, you should honor your body as a creation of God.

The Marvel of Reproduction

Love and devotion between husband and wife is basic

---

[1] Popenoe, Paul, *Building Sex into Your Life*, American Institute of Family Relations, 5287 Sunset Blvd., Los Angeles 27, Calif., p. 22.

to the family. Reproduction of children is a normal result. As Dickerson puts it:

> A child begins to learn early in the home the marvels of reproduction and comes at length to understand and value aright the splendid contribution that sex makes to human life. The child learns much of this just from being reared in a home where a man and a woman live happily as husband and wife and father and mother. From their everyday behavior, more than from what they say, their children learn the meaning of marriage and parenthood and how the sex-linked home partnership may enrich all of one's life. It is no accident that children from happy homes are likely to be good husbands and wives. From infancy they learn by every-day living to understand and appreciate the fine things that are possible because mankind consists of two sexes who may share life as mates in peculiarly satisfying and ennobling ways. It is easy for them to apply in their own marriages what they have been quietly absorbing all their lives in their own homes.[2]

Life Is a Miracle

A mother's contribution to a new life is a tiny speck called a cell. It is so small that two million of them would not fill a thimble. A father's contribution is smaller yet. A million sperm could be packed on a pinhead. Within these cells are still smaller objects called genes, which pass on all the hereditary qualities of father and mother to the children.

When a sperm and egg have united, the tiny speck grows hour by hour into millions of cells that form eyes, ears, brain, muscle, bone and flesh, all properly assembled to form a boy or a girl.

Every birth is a miracle. There is nothing vulgar, cheap or coarse in the kind of creation that makes such a miracle possible. There is nothing about this that parents need to be ashamed of or hesitate to tell their children. Parents are stewards of life. If they view sex in this way—that it is worthy of their stewardship—they lift it above the level of coarse-

2 Dickerson, Roy E., *Home Study Course*, American Institute of Family Relations, Los Angeles, pp. 2, 3.

121

ness to a plane of respect, reverence, awe and even to being an instrument of God in the renewal of life.

Teaching Begins Early

Your first contacts with your new baby involve the body almost entirely. There is cuddling, feeding, changing, bathing. You may look on with amusement as you watch the baby study his fingers, explore his nose, ears, mouth.

During bathing or changing, the baby will discover its sexual parts. When this happens, your amusement can remain amusement, or change quickly to concern. Your own feelings about sex will come into play, and sex education has begun. A tense slap, words like "naughty" or "dirty," a look of repulsion, all are sex education.

Authorities agree that exploration of any part of the body in infancy is simply curiosity. Sexual thoughts are in *your* mind, not the infant's. If you feel that you must divert the child's attention, give him something else to play with. It is important to remember that the organs involving elimination also involve reproduction. You begin to teach attitudes about his body through your manner with the baby while changing or bathing. Remember, God created all of him. Begin teaching him respect for the reproductive system even before he can talk.

At this point it is important to learn correct words so that your child learns to accept the terms genital, navel, urinate as he does toes, hand, eat. Both you and your children need to feel at home with the words and facts which help them understand their bodies.

A short list of essential terms would include these:

Penis—the male organ through which urine and sperm are emitted.

Foreskin—the loose fold of skin which on uncircumcised boys covers the end of the penis.

Circumcision—cutting off of the foreskin as a sanitary measure.

Testicles—male organs suspended in the scrotum.

Scrotum—bag of skin containing the testicles.

122

Breast—in a woman, the organ which makes milk.

Nipple—in a woman, the opening in the breast through which milk is sucked.

Vulva—external parts of female genital organs.

Rectum—lower bowel through which solid waste material passes from the body.

Void or Urinate—discharge urine.

Bowel Movement—elimination of solid wastes.

You Teach Meaning of Intimacy

From the day your child is born, you begin to teach him the meaning of intimacy. Hugging, kissing and patting between husband and wife, or between parent and child, are ways of showing affection rather than for sexual stimulation. Such intimacies are not proper nor socially acceptable toward people who are just acquaintances. An important part of sex education is to teach our children not to bestow their caresses without regard for affection. This teaching is done informally through your own example.

Dickerson has a good comment in this regard:

> It is not sound sex education to encourage any child to be indiscriminate with hugs and kisses. There is no need to discourage a display of affection by those who love him. He needs it and, fortunately, the day is gone when parents were warned against giving it to him. But he needs also, from the very first, to be taught that physical intimacies are fitting only as tokens of regard and affection. Let us begin early to cultivate this feeling and carefully avoid anything which might spoil it. It can be a great protection against the adolescent going in for heavy petting and other intimacies with any convenient person.
>
> Many problems of adolescence might be well-nigh, if not altogether, solved if this healthy minded reserve was carefully nurtured in boys and girls from the very first.[3]

Toilet Training

Toilet training is a process that all parents face with each of their children. This experience is often harder on the

---

[3] Dickerson, *Ibid.*, p. 12.

parent than on the child. Before a child can keep dry and not soil himself, he must develop physically to the point where mind, muscles and nervous system are ready to accomplish the task. Children arrive at this point at different rates of development and age, just as they do in learning to walk.

The parent should remember that the organs involved in toilet training are also sexual organs. You need to be sensible when children show interest in the process or products of elimination. There is no need to become anxious or perturbed during this period. Children will usually proceed at their own rate, no matter what you do. A child who does not soil himself before he has physically arrived at this stage is not advanced. This simply means a meticulous parent, not a trained child.

Teaching Is Continuous

Children express curiosity about human bodies other than their own. They ought to know about bodies, both big and little. This can be done through the normal, everyday processes in the home. You can allow children to satisfy their curiosity while you are taking care of other children through bathing, changing or dressing. When and how much to expose your own body before your children is a more delicate matter. Occasionally, they will wander in while you are dressing or washing. A glimpse of your body at such a time by your youngster is better than the "stolen peek."

Children need to be taught cleanliness, modesty and morality. This is not in conflict with allowing a preschooler to satisfy a normal curiosity. However, each family must be persuaded in their own minds about the line between modesty and curiosity. Training in modesty will start in the toddler years. Children of this age naturally show off and indulge in some sex play. You may glance out the window and see your little girl with her skirt up over her head or a neighbor child in the process of undressing. You may see children examining each other's genitals, especially if

124

they have never seen an undressed person in the home. Boys often go to the toilet in the yard. None of these incidents represent a great crisis. Comparing notes with other parents will show them to be common experiences. When you see these things happen, your opportunity has arrived to start the long process of training in modesty. There is no need to be upset. Healthy, happy children who have reasonable, loving adult supervision will seldom have any long lasting interest in sex play.

When Children Ask

Your preschool child will ask you questions about reproduction. Here are a few universal questions with simple answers:

Where do we get a new baby? It lives and grows inside Mother.

Where does the baby come out? Through a special opening in Mother's body.

How does the baby grow? Mother's body gives it food and keeps it warm. Every day it gets bigger and stronger until it is born.

When the baby kicks, won't it hurt Mother? Babies never kick hard enough to hurt their mothers.

Why do you get so big before you have a baby? Because the baby is growing.

These are typical questions. There are fine books available that will help you to answer your child simply and directly. These may be sex facts to you but they are just simple facts to your child. He is simply wanting to learn. This is your opportunity to begin teaching your child the wonder and majesty of creation. You will need to be prepared for this task. You should be very familiar with the story and with the proper vocabulary.

Having pets around will be helpful in telling the story. There are also books that have been written that small children can understand. Some communities have programs designed to get parents and children talking.

As children grow older they will hear sex talk from school

mates. They will observe many kinds of incidents. They will see pictures in newspapers and magazines and on billboards and television that will raise questions in their minds. They will hear vulgar words. Your attitude and reaction about these things as they come up will determine whether you hear about them again or not. If your response is, "I'll tear the hide off you if I hear you say that again," you probably will not hear it again. If your response is, "Some folks talk that way, but we don't in this family," you will have a better opportunity to build the kind of relationship with your children that will enable you to correct and interpret the experiences your child has outside the home.

Sense of Responsibility

Dr. Popenoe made this provocative statement:

> If [a boy] is to be responsible for his sexual conduct, he must have been made responsible for all other conduct in the past: for picking up his toys, handling his allowance, buying his clothes; for contributing to the welfare of his family in a democratic copartnership; for contributing to the welfare of other families as a junior citizen.[4]

Sex education is not a topic unrelated to the rest of life. The person who must have immediately whatever he wants and have it without regard for anyone else will approach sexual matters in the same way.

Early in the second ten years of life one of the greatest of miracles takes place within the body. This is the maturing of the reproductive system. Here, again, key words are needed to help tell this remarkable story.

Female Reproductive System

Here is a short list regarding the female part of reproduction:

Ovaries—glands which produce eggs and sex hormones.

Uterus—the "womb" in which the baby grows during pregnancy.

---
[4] Popenoe, Paul, *Your Son at Seventeen*, The American Institute of Family Relations, p. 5.

Fallopian Tubes—tubes through which the egg goes on the way from ovary to uterus.

Vagina—a soft muscular passageway leading from the outside of the body to the uterus. It serves as the place of introducing the male sperm into the uterus and as the birth canal for delivery of the baby.

Hymen—a membrane partly closing the entrance to the vagina. It is not present in every female.

Maturation—Development of the female body to the point that a girl can become a mother. This occurs usually between the ages of 10 and 13.

Menstruation—Explained below.

When maturation takes place, the pituitary gland begins to produce a chemical called hormone. This hormone, carried through the blood, stimulates the ovaries to activity. Two things happen when the ovaries become active. First, they produce female sex hormones. These develop the feminine sex characteristics. The breasts begin to develop, the body becomes more curvaceous and the hips broaden. Second, the ovaries begin to produce eggs or ova. These ova mature one at a time and gradually move to the surface of the ovary, forming a blister. When the blister breaks the egg is carried through the Fallopian tube into the uterus. In the meantime, the uterus has been preparing a soft lining to receive the egg. If it does not become fertilized by the male sperm, the lining slowly breaks up into tiny pieces and drains from the uterus, carried by a flow of blood. This process is repeated periodically, gradually taking on a regular cycle of about 28 days. This process is called menstruation—the mark of womanhood.

Now pregnancy is possible. Now stewardship of the body becomes most important. This is a glorious event, not cause for fear and shame.

Male Reproductive System

Some important terms regarding the male part of reproduction are listed:

Sperm—the male seed which fertilizes the female egg.

127

Semen—whitish fluid which contains the sperm.

Vas Deferens—long tube which carries sperm from testicles to seminal vesicles.

Seminal Vesicles—organ which produces semen and carries sperm to prostate.

Prostate Gland—organ which produces part of the material in the semen. It is surrounded by nerves which control erection of the penis.

Urethra—tube which carries semen from prostate to opening of penis. It also carries urine from bladder to penis.

Nocturnal Emission—explained below.

As in the female, the pituitary gland begins to produce a hormone which signals the development of the male reproductive system and male characteristics. This usually occurs between ages 14 and 16. This hormone stimulates the testicles to produce a fluid of their own. Again as in the female, two things happen.

First, bodily changes become apparent. The boy will notice hair growing above the penis, in the armpits and on the legs and face. This fluid causes the voice box, called the larynx, to enlarge with the result that his voice deepens. His shoulders broaden and he becomes more muscular.

Second, the testicles begin to produce millions of sperm. The seminal vesicles produce a milky white fluid which is stored up in the body. In mating, this fluid carrying the sperm passes into the body of the female and, if conditions are right, the sperm fertilizes the female egg to produce a new life.

Occasionally, this fluid passes from the body through the penis at night. This is called a nocturnal emission or wet dream. The youth may wake up while this is happening. If not, he later will find a sticky spot on his pajamas or a starchy circle where the fluid has dried. This is a normal process, like the overflow of a reservoir. It is important that a boy is prepared for this experience and understands the normality of it.

When these changes come, the young man is capable of becoming a father. At this stage, following proper and careful instruction, he will be filled with awe and a sense of stewardship and responsibility of his body.

Reproduction and all that it involves is a marvelous, amazing story. A young person may approach sexual maturity with the feeling that this is a normal development, a part of God's creation to be carefully and reverently managed. Or he may approach these changes with the idea that this is vulgar and dirty, to be hidden as much as possible. It will all depend on his introduction to the process.

CHAPTER II

Preparing your children for marriage

THOSE WHO REMEMBER having gone through adolescence can easily understand that youth in their early teens are very much aware of bodily change.

Along with the development of the reproductive system come noticeable changes in other parts of the body. For the girl, there is the development of the breasts, a broadening of the hips, more curvaceous lines. She undergoes the new experience of menstruation. For the boy, there is the broadening of the shoulders, deepening of the voice, growth of fuzz on his chin.

For both boys and girls there is a spurt in growth and possibly skin eruptions.

This growth and development is irregular. Menstruation

can begin anywhere between the ages of 10 and 16. Growth spurts are early in some youngsters, late in others.

Young people of this age compare themselves a lot with others. Am I normal? How come my younger sister is taller than I am? Why don't I grow as fast as Joe? Look how much faster I am growing than Mary. Look at these big feet, my crooked teeth, my nose, my weight!

Your children must go through this process of discovering their bodies and accepting them for what they are.

Paralleling their preoccupation with their own bodies and comparing themselves with others is a growing awareness of the opposite sex. This is really a gradual process. From the very beginning of life your child has had the pleasurable experience of being held, receiving your caresses and kisses. He sees you, his parents, expressing your regard for each other in the same way. He will realize that touching himself and others is a pleasant experience. Later will come definite pleasurable experiences from tight clothing or pressing up against something like the bar of a bicycle. Sooner or later the child will discover masturbation, an experience that brings with it a mixture of both pleasant and unpleasant feelings.

Somewhere along the path he will discover that being near someone of the opposite sex results in a pleasurable reaction. This knowledge may come quite accidentally, perhaps as casually as a boy and girl sitting together in church. He entered from one side, she from another. They had not planned to sit side by side. Yet, he became pleasantly aware of her presence. Some day, your young person will experience the thrill of his first kiss. He will not soon forget the quick breathing, pounding of his heart and the all-over excitement that tingles in his blood.

TEENS ASK QUESTIONS

Common questions put to me by young people are these: "What's wrong with petting?" "How can I tell when I am in love?"

If their elders would only recognize it, youths who ask

these questions are seeking help in managing a growing attraction toward the opposite sex. The questions come under the circumstance of a natural attraction that is fanned by stimuli from many sides. When such questions come there are often teachable moments, opportunities to teach wholesome attitudes, ideals, convictions.

Petting

What *is* wrong with petting? First of all, petting is intimacy and you parents have the challenge of helping your young people accept intimacy as proper only when it is a token of regard and affection. There is the handshake, the friendly pat on the back, walking arm in arm. These are one thing. The embrace and kiss of greeting, however, is reserved for those who are closely related or who have much in common.

Friends say, "We are very close friends." There is deep enjoyment in being together, sharing the deepest longings of the heart.

Some physical intimacies should be reserved as expressions of deepest love, loyalty and devotion.

Petting, as many young people think of it, is just something to do on a date, like playing ping-pong or bowling—and just as public. Parents should teach children to lift intimacy to the reverent level that God intended for it—a compound of deep love, physical expression, and respect for others.

Self-Control

Second, you can help your teen-ager know that attraction between the sexes is not something that occurs between him and one particular person alone. The attraction can be toward many persons—even a stranger. We often hear of the "strong, unmanageable sex urge." You can remind youth that this urge is unmanageable only when outside influences fan it. Pictures, stimulating reading material, daydreams, conversations and physical contact will fan this urge.

132

Any desire can be fanned. Even the desire for a new car can be fanned to be all-important. You can think about cars, read about them, watch other people drive them. The desire for a car can cause you to do without other things in order to have one. If you want a car badly enough, you will buy it even if it causes strained relations at home.

The sex urge can be fanned in the same way. You can talk about the opposite sex, read about and look at pictures of sex, constantly watch for things that excite you. This is a deliberate effort at keeping the sex urge fanned.

Popenoe[1] gives six reasons why youths are stimulated to sexual intercourse:

1. Curiosity.
2. Desire to feel "grown up."
3. Desire for "adventure."
4. Gang spirit; afraid of being thought a sissy.
5. Anxiety about being abnormal and desire to reassure oneself.
6. Virtual seduction by an older woman.

He adds that authorities who have studied the problems of prostitution declare that boys who frequent houses of ill fame are not driven by an unmanageable urge. Rather, for the most part they are fearful, uneasy, embarrassed, ashamed. Seldom does a teen-ager enter such a place alone. Usually two or more boys go together, egged on by one another.

It is difficult to control sexual passion that has been stimulated. A better way is to avoid the problem. Abigail Van Buren,[2] a popular newspaper problem columnist, has a pithy word for teen-agers:

> Quicker than a penguin sliding down an icicle—that's how quick a necking session can turn into a jam session. And *you're* the one in the jam!

Troubles are like photographs. They are developed in dark

---

[1] Popenoe, Paul, *Building Sex Into Your Life*, The American Institute of Family Relations, Los Angeles, 1944.

[2] Van Buren, Abigail, *Dear Teen-Ager*, Bernard Geis Associates, New York, 1959, pp. 112, 113 and 66, 67.

places. Sitting for hours in a dark room or a parked car and kiss-kiss-kissing is ask-ask-asking for trouble.

Prolonged kissing is . . . the first step in serious love-making. It whets the appetite. It's meant to warm up the engines in preparation for a trip to the moon on gossamer wings. And once the engine is warmed up, it's rugged trying to turn it off. "I couldn't help myself" is the wail in my mail. But my cry in reply is, "Who asked you to warm up the engines?" I can't be more emphatic when I say, "Keep away from tempting situations!" Avoid "overparking." You can get a ticket to some pretty unpleasant places. Double date! . . . Don't invite him over when nobody's home. Stick with the gang on those beach parties. There's safety in numbers.

Girls need to "prove their love" through illicit sex relations like a moose needs a hatrack . . . Clear the cobwebs out of your head: any fellow who asks you to "prove your love" is trying to take you for the biggest, most gullible fool who ever walked. That proving bit is one of the oldest and rottenest lines ever invented!

Does *he* love *you?* It doesn't sound like it. Someone who loves you wants whatever is best for you . . . A boy who loves a girl would sooner cut off his right arm than hurt her.

Self-Control—God's Standard

The Bible speaks out very clearly of God's estimate of sexual relations. Fornication and adultery are sinful. Thus, the advice Miss Van Buren gives makes sense, not just on a logical basis, but spiritually as well.

A discussion of petting can be turned God-ward. The desire to keep His commandments will determine the Christian's behavior. Phyllis McGinley[3] suggests a view that should ring a bell with Christians:

Surely no one would be naive enough to think that little biological chats about conception and bodily structure are sufficient. Our daughters have known for a long time just how babies are born, and have accepted, we hope, their theoretical knowledge of sex gravely and sweetly. But the tides of spring run strong. Home ties are breaking off, and to

3 McGinley, Phyllis, *The Province of the Heart*, The Viking Press, New York, 1959, pp. 35-39.

the confusion of new voices and circumstances and the competition for popularity will be added the pulse of their own blood. Curiosity, even, will have its pull.

. . . What memorable word can we teach them that they can repeat like an incantation if the tide should become a threatening flood? . . . I shall remind my daughters simply that there is such a thing as right and wrong. I shall commit the dreadful heresy of talking about sin . . .

People are no longer sinful; they are only immature or underprivileged or frightened or, more particularly, sick . . . Not once, in any text, did I come across a reference to either right or wrong in regard to the great act of love. Most of the books naturally deplore sexual experimentation. They use all the commonplace arguments. They point out the physical dangers, the emotional involvement, the inconveniences and distresses of furtive passion . . .

Some writers . . . have set down superbly reasoned appeals for chastity. But how strong is reason against a tidal wave? I think conscience proves a superior shelter. My daughters shall be told there exists a moral law and an ancient commandment and they do wrong to flout them . . . I should like to argue the wholesomeness of treating extramarital relations as sinful . . . to begin with, sin implies goodness, and the young love goodness with all their hearts. We all know what idealists they are, how fiercely they react against injustice and cruelty, how they hate hypocrisy and cant. To take away their delight in virtue, to tell them that they must withstand temptations because temptations are merely urges toward immature behavior, is to give them stones when they pant for bread. It is to weaken the muscles of their characters.

. . . So what in the end shall I tell my daughters about chastity before marriage? Of *course,* I shall be sensible and point out the ordinary social penalties attached to any other conduct. I shall touch on the possible pregnancy, the untidiness, the heartbreak. But I shall also say that love is never merely a biological act but one of the few miracles left on earth, and that to use it cheaply is a sin.

When Is It Love?

A second question often asked is, How do I know it is love?

Signs of Love

Some years ago in a lecture, Dr. Roy E. Dickerson, nationally-known social worker, told of a couple who approached him. Both were seriously puzzled. They were considering marriage, but were not sure they were in love. Neither was in a daze. There were no dizzy spells and the thrill between them was not very noticeable.

However, he said, they did exhibit these signs of love:

1. Abiding sense of comradeship. Sweethearts are pals. They enjoy being together, more with each other than anyone else, although others are not excluded from their lives. When they are absent from each other, each is in the background of the other's thoughts. There is an eagerness to understand one another. They get satisfaction from a "we" feeling. While giving-in can be done in a nasty, reluctant way, these two show a spirit of mutual thoughtfulness.

2. Feeling that life has been lifted to higher levels. They inspire each other to new hopes, new virtues, honor and loyalty, all of this providing them a stability.

3. Putting sex feelings in perspective. Ordinarily there is a stirring of sexual desire. This is not uncleanness. The reaction will be to curb, to control, to manage this desire. Any caressing will be an expression of devotion and loyalty. It will be handled in such a way that it will not impair the relationship. Love curbs the crude and selfish.

Premarital relations are no measure of sexual adjustment. Complete mutuality is not achieved for months after marriage. In fact, premarital experience can be completely misleading. Relations within marriage are respectable and decent. Outside of marriage there is guilt, shame, loss of respect. It spoils the relationship.

One girl had premarital relations with her boy friend and broke up with him. She met another man whom she greatly respected. What should she do? Tell him? She did not want to be a cheat and she was afraid gossip would get to him.

One couple were having relations. He was killed in an accident a week before the wedding.

In another instance, the fellow was drafted. They became suspicious and distrustful of each other.

4. Self-restraint. The young person who thinks he is in love may well ask himself: Do we become easily impatient with each other? Any two persons will have differences and may discuss them heatedly. The test is whether they use words with intent to hurt the other one.

Constant quarreling without solving anything will not suddenly change after the ceremony. Some men have the idea that there is no need for sexual restraint after marriage. Actually, there will be times when illness or excessive demands on the wife will require long-term restraint.

5. Similarity of ideals. One man was a Presbyterian; his friend a Christian Scientist. They were fond of each other. But they decided not to marry because he could not stand the thought of no medical attention for his children.

Some try to combat such differences by putting religion outside their consideration. Young people should not bank on being exceptions to the rule of similarity when it comes to ideals.

6. Love of children. Most marriages produce children. This is one of the main purposes and to some the main purpose of sexual relations. Unless the couple can reach a mutual viewpoint on the place they want children to occupy in their home, their unity is threatened from the very outset.

7. Confidence and trust. Two persons in love learn they can count on one another at all times.

To help their children answer the question, "How do I know I am in love?" the Christian parent can supply information that the young person may easily overlook.

Love or Lust?

1. A difference. You can point out that in this day, there is great confusion in terms. We identify lust with love. A lad may say, "I had a girl out last night and loved her up a lot." A headline in the paper will read, "Two Die Keeping Love Tryst." We are bombarded all day long by records,

radio and television with songs that identify love with passion and lust.

If you pick up almost any magazine and newspaper you will find advertisements that suggest their products further romance, and embracing is usually the symbol. The best-seller books often leave little to the imagination.

It was amazing to get a circular from a Christian supply house that promised with the purchase of a Bible they would send a record on marriage that would help one discover "the fun and excitement of life's most thrilling adventure."

In our younger days, the song, "That Old Feeling" was popular. It describes love as a heart-stopping thrill when "you" go by. The suggestion is that if the sight of a certain person "thrills" you, it must be love.

You must recognize that at the very time your young people are becoming aware of a natural attraction toward the opposite sex, they are being hit from all sides by the notion that passion and thrill are love. Romance is depicted as a tingling, passionate, thrilling experience.

Now add the normal sexual attraction between male and female to this emphasis on "falling in love" and the stage is set for the emotional tangles that many youth get into.

Psychologists call this infatuation. It is a physical attraction based on looks, fun to be with, even held together against their better judgment, not based on a state of respect and comradeship that develops when there are similar ideas, tastes and hopes.

2. Similarities. You can teach your children that love, in spite of the constant emphasis, does not need to stand the test of passion. A better test is on similarities shared.

More than 100 studies show that the more alike two persons are, the better will be their chance for an enduring marriage. "Opposites attract" is a much-believed axiom. Perhaps it is true in some phases of physical science, but not in marriage. Similarities in upbringing, education, religion, race and even economic levels are to be desired for couples getting married.

138

Marriages mixing religious faiths are particularly difficult to work out. It is the position of the Roman Catholic Church that the marriage ceremony be performed by a Catholic clergyman, that the non-Catholic promise his children will be baptized and brought up as Catholics, that he or she promise not to interfere with the religious practices of the partner who is a Catholic.

Should the Christian youth holding to an evangelical standard expect a lesser demand from his own faith? Mixed marriages at best are compromises. It is important that parents take an interest in their children's friends. The Christian, to be sure that his child will marry one of like faith, must see that his children associate with such people.

In order for this to be possible, it is important that the church provide adequate facilities and an adequate program that will attract and hold youth. At this point, the parents who have not neglected their roles as churchmen

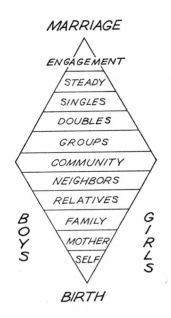

THE DATING LADDER

will be greatly rewarded. Equally important is the type of fellowship that the family enjoys. If the family associates primarily with non-Christians, it is not strange if the children's friends are mostly non-Christians.

3. A charted path. You can help youth see the pathway that leads from birth to marriage.

David Treat, the health educator of Flint, Mich., has devised what he calls a dating ladder to depict the steps a child takes in his development from birth to marriage.

Not all children will go through all these steps. In general, the infant, at first preoccupied with himself, will gradually recognize and respond to his mother, then his family, and more slowly, come to include a wide circle of the community, including friends at school, church and wherever else he has contacts. The child may have a fondness for someone his or her own age. He may intensely like someone his own sex, but much older, like the Scoutmaster, a Sunday School teacher or a hero in the headlines. He may develop a crush on someone of the opposite sex, but much older. This may be a national figure, a neighbor, a teacher.

Soon there will be group activities involving both sexes. Parties, outings, hikes provide such contacts. Suddenly, the child will discover the opposite sex. Boys will view girls from a distance, talk about them, tease them, push and shove them. Then will begin the process of pairing off, doubly perhaps at first, then single dating, going steady and finally engagement and marriage.

4. Wholesome individuals. If the statistics are true, today's youth must learn to establish themselves as wholesome individuals. This includes wholesome relations with both sexes. It ought to be obvious that picking a mate is only half the matter. Can we help them to see that happiness in marriage results not so much from finding the right person as from *becoming* the right person?

Limitless books and articles have been written to help youth in their development, how to be liked and the route to becoming a mature person. There is no wiser advice, however, than that found in the Bible:

Thou shalt love thy neighbor as thyself (Matt. 22:39).
Whosoever will be great among you, let him be your minister (Matt. 20:26).
And whosoever of you will be the chiefest, shall be servant of all. For even the Son of man came not to be ministered unto, but to minister, and to give his life a ransom for many (Mark 10: 44-45).
Be kindly affectioned one to another with brotherly love; in honor preferring one another (Rom. 12:10).

Yes, a vital task of a young person is to become a mature, genuine, real person who can be rightly related to others. To be yourself, to learn to meet changes and to develop is a priceless lesson to learn. Pretense blurs the picture of a person and makes congenial relations almost impossible. The highest goal to achieve is summarized in these words:

But grow in grace, and in the knowledge of our Lord and Saviour Jesus Christ. To him be glory both now and forever. Amen (II Pet. 3:18).

Summary 3

Parenthood launches the couple on an irreversible way of life. As children grow, they make relentless demands on the energy and ingenuity of their parents. But children grow up in a reasonably systematic way, enabling the parent to become familiar with what to expect. A study of the developmental tasks of family living will help the parent to anticipate stages so he may help his children achieve healthy growth.

Discipline is everything that you do in order to train your child in the way that he should go. Undergirding the process is the spirit of love, which we have referred to as "the spectrum of love." The major task is to teach the child a wholesome fear of God and a love for His precepts. The tools for training are knowledge of the needs of children, knowledge of the particular child, definite limits, willingness to help the child with your personal supervision.

From early in life, the child is confronted with the complexities of his physical self. As a Christian, you ought to have the greatest respect and admiration for your own body, the creation of God. In giving "due benevolence" to your marriage partner you will be teaching your child about sex. You ought to look forward to the privilege of telling your children the marvelous story of creative life.

As your children grow older, they will become conscious of the differences between men and women and will be attracted to the opposite sex. Your task here is a most serious one—to help your children develop wholesome attitudes, high Christian standards and an understanding of genuine love. The objective will be to assist your children to become the persons that will bring to their own marriages the qualities that will make them truly Christian.

After launching your children into marriage, your own home remains. The nest is empty now, just like when you began. How you have prepared for the empty nest will determine what kind of life remains for you.

CHAPTER 12

Taking an over-all view

WE HAVE GIVEN our views on the task called marriage. Now let us look back on what has been said to get a panoramic view.

Reviewing the elements of marriage and a family brings to mind a personal experience in mountain climbing. With three companions we stood at the top of a glacier, astounded at the breath-taking view eight thousand feet below. There was a solemn quietness at the top. What a thrill, what joy, what a sense of accomplishment in achieving the summit. We stood speechless, drinking in the vastness of the wide world at our feet.

It had been an eight-hour climb over unfamiliar, rugged terrain. Poorly fitting shoes had caused several blisters. A fall, ending on a rock, netted a painful bruise. One hand throbbed with pain because it had grabbed hold of a thorny branch. At one point we came to a sheer cliff. A more experienced member of the party started up. We watched, uncertainly. Loose boulders came hurtling past us and bounced on to the base of the mountain. But our friend made it and we were encouraged to climb.

Once there was a steep snowfield to cross. Slipping and sliding made our hearts race wildly and it took courage even to move. Then came long, shady trails, covered with soft, cool moss and lined with great timbers. Swift, clear streams and lacy waterfalls were close by.

At last, we reached the summit—tired, aching, hungry, but victorious, satisfied. It was worth the effort. We were happy.

Many persons have looked up at those gleaming, snow-capped peaks and that glacier, which seemed so near, so accessible, so inviting. Some have started out to conquer them, filled with enthusiasm and purpose. But the climb upward has filled them with fear. The miles have proved disappointing and disheartening. The distance is greater than anticipated, the ascent much steeper. They have become utterly unappreciative of the quiet valleys, the great trees, the roaring rapids and mighty waterfalls. Instead, they have become increasingly aware of tired muscles, sore feet, exhaustion, dampness. Somewhere along the way, facing a particularly difficult grade, courage has faltered, purpose has died. It is time to reconsider the goal. Sadly, they have given up. They have turned around and limped home. These were unprepared or unwilling to face the obstacles.

The successful ones, starting out on the same journey, have found pleasure and challenge in the very roughness and hardness of the journey. They have found joy in the same difficulties that overwhelmed the others. The struggle up the mountain has become rewarding, though exhausting. Success in mastering a slope inspired courage and hope for tackling the next one.

Mountain climbing consists of beautiful vistas, long periods of uninteresting, undesirable stretches, bracing air, steep and difficult places, danger, strain, pain, co-operation. Mountain climbers depend on each other, sustain, pull up and boost each other. The demands and dependence on one another build a bond of friendship among the climbers —or they can cause rifts and conflicts to develop.

This summit view affords an appraising look at marriage. All who marry start out hand in hand with their hopes high, joyously, with lively, eager anticipation. As they look up the trail, a life together, establishing a home, raising a family all beckon. It all seems so easy to attain, so inviting. You will remember Ken and Pat in our opening chapter. Soon after being married, he discovered that she snored. They became at odds over the tempo their life together should take. They had arrived at the first steep climb in their marriage and the summit did not then seem so easy to reach. But they both are sincere Christians and they turned to God for wisdom and strength to solve these problems. They found a solution and through it learned of the help that God can give a couple, including the renewed hope and courage needed to face the next challenge.

Not so with Wally and Marge. He insists that she is not neat enough around the house. She says her appearance behind closed doors is her own business. Wally wants Marge to care for the flowers and shrubs, but complains that she spends too much money in doing so. Her reply? Do it yourself, mister. Before the first real rise in the trail is reached, their progress forward has slackened and they have begun to complain.

Preparation for marriage consists of two important commitments: First, to love God with all your heart, soul and mind, and, second, to keep His commandments.

God would have you love all men with a love that has at least nine components: Patience, kindness, generosity, humility, courtesy, unselfishness, good temper, guilelessness and sincerity.

Two persons who set out to love each other in this way— which Drummond calls the "spectrum of love"—sooner or later discover that man alone is incapable of loving another person in this way and that he cannot live up to such virtues before God.

They are all gone out of the way, they are together become unprofitable; there is none that doeth good, no, not one (Rom. 3:12).

But fortunate are those who have acknowledged that they are weak and inadequate and who have discovered that in Jesus Christ lies the strength and courage necessary for their journey. As Paul the apostle put it:

. . . but though our outward man perish, yet the inward man is renewed day by day. For our light affliction, which is but for a moment, worketh for us a far more exceeding and eternal weight of glory; While we look not at the things which are seen, but at the things which are not seen: for the things which are seen are temporal; but the things which are not seen are eternal (II Cor. 4:16-18).

It is the spiritual man who is renewed day by day: renewed in comfort and consolation (II Cor. 1:3-5), in patience and joy (Col. 1:11), wisdom (James 1:5), righteousness (Phil. 3:9) and in peace and hope (Rom. 15:13).

The serious Christian couple, recognizing their need of Christ as Saviour and source of renewed life, will not be overwhelmed by the stresses and strains of the journey. Their mutual objective is to please God and to serve Him. As they master one obstacle after another, through the grace of Christ, they can say with increasing certainty what Isaiah said:

For the Lord God will help me; therefore shall I not be confounded; therefore have I set my face like a flint, and I know that I shall not be ashamed (Isa. 50:7).

The journey along the marital trail requires careful balance, lest you tumble headlong into disaster. Men must balance their roles as husband, father, employer or employee, son, churchman, among others. For the women, there are the roles of wife, mother, daughter, churchwoman. For both, there is the vital role of being a person. The world is a fascinating place and offers many interesting things to do. But to keep your life in a proper, healthy balance, careful study and often sacrifice are required.

146

A wholesome marriage also requires good will, co-operation, dedication. It implies two free people who voluntarily make their way on the same trail, with the husband taking the lead. The spirit permeating a wholesome marriage is beautifully described by Paul:

> Now I beseech you, brethren, by the name of our Lord Jesus Christ, that ye all speak the same thing, and that there be no divisions among you; but that ye be perfectly joined together in the same mind and in the same judgment (I Cor. 1:10).

Those who must have their own way find these requirements too steep, their steps falter and they consider turning back.

Marriage is not like walking along a familiar trail that you have explored many times and for which you know every twist and turn along the way. Marriage, rather, is more like a strange trail with every turn holding something new. There are pleasant stretches easily mastered. Then, there are steep, rugged places which leave you aching and exhausted. One fact in life is certain: "the certainty of uncertainty." The mature Christian makes his way along the trail with keen interest, enjoying the variety and the unexpected and getting satisfaction out of meeting the challenges. A new baby in the family, a promotion, a move into another house, sickness, death, accidents, a new responsibility in the church, new friends—these are some of the changes that come into a family's life.

Each change, with the problems that it brings, exposes the soul. In decision making, your values and goals come into play. We have the promise:

> The meek will he guide in judgment: and the meek will he teach his way (Ps. 25:9).

Such a man can gather the facts, sift them and come to a decision that will be according to God's way.

There are many natural changes that come to a married couple. You pass from the family founding stage to the child-bearing, child-rearing, child-launching, the empty nest.

An endless shelf of books has been written to describe these stages. In our day, we need not be taken by surprise by the nature of parenthood. For each of these stages Havighurst aptly describes the growth process as a series of "developmental tasks." He defines a developmental task as one which "arises at or about a certain period in the life of an individual, successful achievement of which leads to his happiness and to success with later tasks, while failure leads to unhappiness in the individual, disapproval by the society and difficulty with later tasks."

Familiarity with these stages can be acquired. It involves purpose, vision, effort. The resources are available and can be mastered by the mature person. Guiding a child, then, through the various stages involves knowledge, maturity, certainty. The task is described in Proverbs 22:6:

> Train up a child in the way he should go: and when he is old, he will not depart from it.

Training, or discipline, includes everything you do in order to help the child learn. It involves the home, school, church and other agencies. It is a twenty-year process. The major task is to teach your children from the beginning that you are followers of the Master, that they need Christ as Saviour, that they should keep God central in their lives, that you look for the return of Christ.

Guiding children involves a purpose and a goal. Parents must assume responsibility for influencing children and making their learning good and effective. As you study the job you will find you have made mistakes. But dedicated, purposeful loving effort will enable you to correct those mistakes. Failure to prepare for and understand the stages of a child's growth and your own as well will cause progress along the trail to be most difficult.

As your children grow, you have the important task of teaching them a sense of reverence and awe toward their own bodies and their God-given power to pass life on to someone else. You will do this in simple ways. Your attitude about the body will be taught as you cuddle the child,

148

bathe him, go through the toilet training process and give him answers to his questions. The relationship between you and your partner will contribute greatly to his concept of how a man and woman should treat each other.

As the child becomes aware of the opposite sex, he should understand the normality of this attraction, the value of careful management of it, the importance of physical contact being an expression of the deepest love, loyalty and devotion. A mature, genuine, wholesome person, rightly related to others and to God, is ready to choose a mate and go on to found his own family.

When the last child has been launched, you and your partner will face a new challenge. This should be a great day, bringing with it a sense of accomplishment. If you have given your best to the job, you will enter the empty-nest stage with the satisfaction of a job well done.

We may liken the beginning of the empty-nest stage to arriving at the summit after a long climb up the mountain. This is the top. What joy at being here. True, all trails lead downward. But the couple at the summit soon realize that the trail down tugs on a set of muscles other than those used on the way up. It takes energy and effort to get down from the top. And as on the upward trail, there are pleasant places and danger spots on the way down.

When a couple's nest becomes empty, they still have important tasks to look forward to. Success in this stage will depend on your preparation for it. Your approach to past stages will no doubt be a good indication of how you will approach this one. The basic requirements are the same—love, unity, dedication to God. The specific tasks involved include resuming your life as a couple, developing a new relationship with your children (and learning how to get on with your grandchildren), use of more leisure time, decreasing physical strength, retirement, perhaps reduced income.

Preparation will involve study, careful planning, effort.

Sooner or later will come the day that all travelers look forward to with keen anticipation and joy—the time when the end of the trail is reached. It will not be so important that the journey was less difficult and trying than others before you experienced. Of prime importance will be the fact of getting there, that you have held true to the course, that you have achieved your clearly defined objectives.

Let us go to Paul one last time:

> And to be found in him, not having mine own righteousness, which is of the law, but that which is through the faith of Christ, the righteousness which is of God by faith: That I may know him, and the power of his resurrection, and the fellowship of his sufferings, being made conformable unto his death; If by any means I might attain unto the resurrection of the dead (Phil. 3:9-11).

The one who can look back on a lifetime of preparation for this day can anticipate the same reception that the servant received when his lord returned after a long absence:

> Well done, thou good and faithful servant: thou hast been faithful over a few things, I will make thee ruler over many things: enter thou into the joy of thy lord (Matt. 25:21).

Index

Adjustment, faulty approach, 34; involved in marriage, 8; involved in restoration, 72; necessary for wife, 55

Adolescent, *See* Youth

Adulthood, early (age 18 to 30), 99-100; later, 100; middle (age 30 to 55), 100

Altar, family, *See* Devotions, family

Appreciation, *See* Praise and admonition

Attitude, component of maturity, 22; how expressed, 66; in discipline, 105; in goal, 30; in sex education, 119-120, 122; Schindler definition of, 22; toward church, 37; toward things, 36; toward this world, 33

Authority, disrespect for, 112; God-given, 107; imbued with love, 46; in decision making, 89-90

Balance, for marriage partners, 8; in roles, 41-43, 47, 51

Barnhouse, Donald Grey, 74, 83

Behavior, child's, 112; conduct from heart, 24; covering up sin, 32; in sexual relations, 134; similarities in, 17; uncertain indicator, 23-24

Beliefs and convictions, and change, 78, 83; and roles, 43; dynamic kernel, 19; great differences in, 17; in decision making, 89; underlying communication, 69; why Christian necessary, 25; *See also* Values

Believer's state, 82

Bible, and discipline, 109; as guidebook, 9, 13-16; as mirror, 31; as source book, 31; benefits of, 30; essential in knowing God's will, 107; illustrations, facing pages 16 and 96; in family

devotions, 116-117; interpretation of, 5; on communication, 67; study of required, 16; teaching on solution to man's problems, 22; will not pass away, 82-83

Big Brother movement, 45

Body, human, changes, 127, 128, 130-131; child's curiosity of, 124; creation of God, 120; great miracle, 119

Bossard, James H. S., 66, 67, 69

Bourdeau, Hugo A., 65, 67, 68

Brandt, Henry R., 45

Building a Christian Home, organization of book, 5

Change, certain to come, 73; challenge to parents, 102; continuous, 85; in marriage circumstances, 12; in parental tasks, 100; prayer on, 85; universal, 76; *See also* Believer's state, Creation, Death, Economics, Environment, Separation, Sickness, Unchanging principles

Children, agreement on, 137; development from birth, 139, 140; infant, 96-97, 98-99; middle childhood (age 6 to 12), 97, 99; younger years, 97, 98-99, 124-125; *See also* Needs of children

Choice, between good activities, 42; involved in marriage, 8

Christ, atoning death remedy for sin, 23; belief in as Saviour, 17; benefits of relationship to, 23; center of life, 50; child's need of, 106; love supplies grace, 56; return looked for, 25-27, 33; source of strength, courage and renewed life, 146; substitutionary sacrifice, 5, 22; transforms the heart, 24

151

Christian, beliefs, *See* Doctrinal statements; definition of, 5; life centered on Christ, 50; a servant and witness, 37

Church, The, as a help to parents, 102; attitude toward, 37; dedication to demonstrated, 48-49; holding young people, 139; Roman Catholic and evangelical views of marriage, 139; source of workers, 37

Churchman, 48-49, 139

Citizen, 49

Clara Elizabeth Fund, 6, 95

Communication, based on beliefs, 69; causes of breakdown in, 67-69; channels of, 62; high premium on, 61; matter of spirit, 70; necessary to happy marriage, 66; not enough in itself, 68; results, 72; stopped by concealment *(which see)*, 66; type of, 71-72

Compromise, 54

Comradeship, 136

Concealment (tendency to hide), 68, 70; cause of, 69; overcome by communication, 61; stronger than unity, 66

Conversation, 65-66, 67, 69

Conviction (confidence), for family devotions, 116; in discipline, 108, 109-110, 115

Couple, 58-59; in empty nest, 149

Courtesy, 10, 115

Creation, 82

Cultural activities, 26

Cycle, family, *See* Development

Dating ladder, 139, 140

Death, 78-79

Decision and decision making, binding, 89; continuous stream of, 85; made by husband, 53-54; power given to child gradually, 110; reversed, 111; stalemate over, 89

Desire, to do good, 19-20, 24-25; *See also* Frustration

Development, family, stages in, 95-96; mother's, 109; understanding of youngster's, 108; uneven progress in, 101

Developmental task, at various ages, 98-100; definition of, 98

Devotions, family, 116-117

Dickerson, Roy E., 6, 121, 123, 136

Discipline, and family devotions, 116-117; and God, 106-107; as guidance, 104; as punishment, 103; conviction in, 109-110; definition of, 104-105; foundation for, 105-106; help in, 112-113; illustration, facing page 96; involves knowledge, 108-109; limits in, 111-112; pressure against resistance, 113-116; supervision in, 110-111

Divorce, 80, statistics on, 68

Doctrinal statements, 22-23, 25-26

Drummond, Henry, 10

Due benevolence, 119-120

Economics, attitude toward, 36; change in, 80; in goal, 26; place of money, 47; spending on church, 48

Employee and employer, 46-47

Empty nest, 58, 59; illustration, facing page 113; tasks of, 149

English and Pearson, 20, 22

Environment, 81-82

Eternity, as goal, 30; in mature thinking, 33; lose sight of, 36; makes a difference, 29

Faith, 78, 79; in decision making, 91

Fakkema, Mark, 106

Family, after death of father, 78-79; associates of, 139-140; challenge for, 63; raising of, 101; typical American, 18

Father, 45-46; death of, 78-79

Fellowship, 63

Foundation, Christ's views on, 14; elements of, 9, 70; for communication, 69; for discipline, 105; for marriage, 8; for prob-

female system, 126-127; terms of male system, 127-128; *See also* Growth; Body, human

Reproof, 71-72

Responsibility, child's awareness of, 97; for sex conduct, 126; husband's and wife's clarified, 53; husband's delegation to wife, 44; husband's in home, 44; in decision making, 90; in discipline, 109; in parenthood, 96; in training and raising new life, 119; relinquishing to child, 104; to God as parents, 107-108

Restoration, 71-72

Righteousness, 23; guide to, 30, 31; in communication, 71-72; keep child in, 103-104

Roles, in decision making, 89-90, 92; illustration, facing page 32; of the man, 42; of the woman, 51; *See also* Churchman, Citizen, Employee or Employer, Father, Homemaker, Husband, Mother, Neighbor, Person, Relative, Son or Son-in-law, Wife

St. Paul, 24

Schindler, John A., 20, 22

Selfishness, 89

Separation, 80

Sex, awareness of opposites, 131-132, 140; differences become manifest, 97; extramarital relations as sin, 134-135; feelings in perspective, 136; high plane of relations, 119; intimacy, 123; masturbation, 127, 130-131; menstruation, 131; nocturnal emission, 128; passion, control of, 133-134; petting, 132-135; problems clear up, 119; self-control, 132; "unmanageable urge," 132-133; *See also* Sex education

Sex education, definition of, 118; essential terms, 122, 126-127 (female), 127-128 (male); illus-tration, facing page 97; modesty, 124-125; parental influence in, 120, 121; questions and answers, 125; toilet training, 123-124; when to begin, 122; *See also* Reproduction, human

Sickness, 79-80

Similarities, test for love, 138-139

Sin, Biblical view of, 19-20; covering, result of, 24; frustration caused by, 21-22; McGinley on, 134-135; rid by atoning work of Christ, 32; sacrifice for, 5; view on it helps shape outlook, 19

Sinner, 5

Son or son-in-law, 48

"Spectrum of Love," application of, 11; components, 10, 70; in discipline, 105; in relationships, 13

Spiritual fruit, *See* Fruit of the Spirit

Stability, 136; guide to, 30, 32; secret of, 33; *See also,* Unchanging principles

Standard, children want, 116; husband sets, 45; in discipline, 105; many opinions on, 64; mutually acceptable, 71; of self-control, 134

Submission, freedom comes through, 54; not end of freedom, 56; to Spirit of God, 5; to unreasonable husband, 56; what warranted by, 45

Supervision, and discipline, 110-111; and sex education, 125

Task, developmental, *See* Developmental Task

Teachable moment, for differing age levels, 101; favorable time for learning, 98; must identify, 102; when questions arise, 132

Teen-agers, *See* Youth

Toilet training, *See* Sex education

Training of children, *See* discipline

Treat, David B., 6, 95, 120, 140